SUPERSPILL

SUPERSPILL

The Future of
Ocean Pollution

James Dawson

JANE'S

LONDON · NEW YORK · SYDNEY

Copyright © 1980 James Dawson

First published in the United Kingdom in 1980 by
Jane's Publishing Company Limited,
238 City Road,
London EC1V 2PU

ISBN 0 7106 0064 x

Published in the United States of America in 1981 by
Jane's Publishing Incorporated
730 Fifth Avenue
New York
N.Y. 10019

ISBN 0 531 03709 6

Typesetting by D. P. Media Limited, Hitchin, Hertfordshire

Printed in Great Britain by
Redwood Burn Limited
Trowbridge and Esher

Contents

Illustrations, Maps, Tables

Dedication

To a true friend of many years standing, Willard Bascom, Oceanographer and inventor/innovator of many underwater systems, including dynamically positioned ships. He introduced me to this fascinating field many years ago and changed the course of my life.

Preface

Oil has been maturing for aeons of time. We pull out the corks and carelessly swill and spill the precious liquids and gases as if it was water from an ever bubbling spring, recycled by rainfall.

The well managed oil tanker fleets proclaim how great is their skill and how small is the percentage of hydrocarbons spilled in the ocean, compared to that actually carried by ships. Their records of spillage are small, but the smaller owners hiring their ships to larger companies are responsible for spills that are becoming catastrophic both in their size, extent and frequency.

Add to this the fact that the charts of the world's seas were mostly made by lead and line in the nineteenth century from ships with draughts, like the first oil tanker, of 23 feet, and the dangers at sea begin to be revealed. Today keels are common at depths of 50 to 80 feet.

Until Masters and Officers with records of incompetence are exposed quickly after an "accident", nothing will improve the staggering increase in loss of life both human and animal, and the loss of ever scarcer fuels from dwindling sources under the earth's crust will continue.

We cannot afford another decade of waste and fouling of the oceans and legislators must look at the horizon and not at the voters at their feet.

Introduction

My naval service in World War II included six months at sea in a British anti-aircraft cruiser, H.M.S. *Dido*, in the Mediterranean. During that time it was mooted that the ship's quick-firing 5.25-in high-angle guns downed more friendly planes than enemy ones. This startling gap in communication between allies and friendly forces, a characteristic of all wars before and after, led inevitably to a request of their Lordships of the Admiralty for me to serve as a Naval Air Liaison Officer. The function of this appointment was to prevent the Army and Air Force warring with the Navy and each other. The theatres of operations were the Mediterranean, Aden and thus the Indian Ocean and the Bay of Bengal from Ceylon, India and Burma.

When peace came, and swords were being fashioned into plough-shares, the experience of disentangling friendly forces locked in lethal embrace proved valuable to a returning Marine Insurance Broker, at Lloyd's of London. I had worked there from school leaving age in 1940, until I was caught in the draft in late 1941. These two years of broking American ships crossing the Atlantic, through wolf packs of enemy submarines and the mighty *Bismarck*, were to stand me in good stead when breadlines snaked over Europe, exhausted by six years of war.

The reason for specialising in the insurance of undersea risks lies elsewhere. But the subject is so wide and so fascinating, peopled by so few specialists, that it seemed natural to "join the Club" and become an oceanographer on the way.

Propulsion into this field was supplied by a Great Grandfather, who was Principal of McGill University during its most formative years (1853 to 1895), and two Grandfathers severally Geographer of Canada and "Father of Canadian Tidal and Current Investigations on the Atlantic and Pacific Coasts". In 1888, nearly 400 Captains and Ship's officers joined a petition to the Ottawa Government for surveys of the hazardous East Coast of Canada, which if undertaken "serious loss of life and property due to shipwrecks attributed to unknown currents during fogs and hazy weather, may thus be greatly diminished". My Grandfather, William Bell Dawson, accepted the job of Engineer in charge of the Tidal Survey. He asked for a modest $29,000 to undertake this Herculean job, and was voted only a third of this amount.

The operations had to be conducted by a tiny hard-pressed staff, using lead-lines tossed from a refitted tugboat, from sailing gigs, or from open dories.

Added to my enthusiasm for the sea kindled by my Grandfather, I had a number of naval uncles and naval godfather. My love for the sea emerged from boyhood, strong and not to be seduced by other interests, and was tinged with awe when I first saw storms and the power of wind and wave in the North Atlantic in winter.

Practical interest in hydrography was illuminated by my looking at a chart of Hudson's Bay and learning the meaning of a circle of black dots looking very lonesome on the white chart. Each dot represented a sounding by lead and line. I realised, without much insight, that what was each side of the dot . . . a rock, a pinnacle . . . was unknown to the cartographer, much less to modern seafarers using these nautical charts.

The five years following my illumination were an engrossing study of the number of ships that grounded every day, culled from the oldest daily newspaper in the world, *Lloyd's List*, first published in 1734.

Over a three year period, I discovered that an average of three-and-a-half ships a day ran aground, touched the ground, or were wrecked. One of the fastest growing industries is naming rocks after the ships that strike them. When this study was completed, I took the matter up with the world's hydrographers, past and present, and both parties received a considerable jolt to previously held notions. It soon became apparent, when the Hydrographers in Monaco, London, Washington, Ottawa and elsewhere were consulted, that the fault did not lie, in most cases, with the mid-eighteenth-century charts, but with ships' Masters and Navigators ignoring common-sense advice in the Pilot books available to all, and not treating the charts as open to interpretation. The energetic and effective British Government Hydrographer, said at a recent seminar . . . "I think it absolutely vital that the user should know how accurate the information on a chart is, and one way is to look at the date. If it was done by a sailing ship in 1840, you obviously don't take your ship very close to a charted shoal, or you navigate with caution through the area. Unless the source data diagram is on the chart, and you can see that you are in an area which has not been surveyed for 140 years, you sail in blissful ignorance of the dangers." That advice springs from a true seaman, with the blood of Nelson and Matthew Maury in his veins. But his pearls of commonsense and wisdom do not reach the ears of those who must heed them, and are only listened to by the already converted. They are all exasperated and frustrated as they observe the chaos at sea resulting in so many groundings, strandings and collisions, mostly in coastal waters.

1. "Superspill – The Future of Ocean Pollution"

The terror of a lee shore is the most awesome in the range of dangers facing any seafarer worth his salt. Anyone conscious of this vital chemical in his blood has been stirred by paintings depicting sailing ships at the point of destruction under cliffs and on dark rocks lashed by mountainous seas.

Lee shores are just as much a menace to present day ships both great and small, but modern imagination has been obscured by the massive size of present day oil carriers. A large oil tanker in expert hands is difficult to manoeuvre at all times, in any circumstances, but a lee shore is no place for a helpless ship of 363,000 tons carrying 220,000 tons of light Arabian crude oil. Pulling such a massive structure, the largest moving objects made by man, against galeforce head winds to safety, is a job for experts who are aware of the shortening odds against successful salvage, dictated by rising seas and narrowing sea room. There is little time for even the nimblest-minded captain to measure his options when beset by storm winds and waves and machinery failure. These circumstances, fraught with a variety of decisions, any one of which may lead to the sudden end of a long career at sea, render the translation of responsibility far from the site of the crisis a strong enticement to a captain facing disaster.

The Master and crew of sailing ships wallowing helplessly towards towering cliffs hear the wind whistling in the shrouds and the boom of bellying canvas mixed with the roar of seas bursting onto the cliffs that tower over them.

The Master and crew of a helpless 300,000-ton oil tanker, remote from this noise and fear, in a white capsule surrounded by automated navigational aids, are not stimulated into a life preserving flow of adrenalin. The feeling of remoteness, high above the waves, gives an impression of omnipotence, standing on the bridge of a ship some 1,000 feet long. The reality of approaching destruction, on rocks and hidden by storm driven ways, is quite remote. None of the sounds and violent movement familiar to seamen, since Henry the Navigator sent his ships south into the unknown from Sagres, along the African Coast, are heard or felt in today's big ships. Movement in large tankers in lively or lumpy seas is dulled from jerky uplift and sickening plunge, to a mere undulation. Robbed of these inducements to survival, seamen in these huge structures feel no sense of imminent danger, nor the sting of wind blown spume that excites seamen to make urgent steps to avoid destruction.

If the Master's sense of the onset of disaster is absent, his reaction is to pass responsibility elsewhere and in the case of the *Amoco Cadiz* the Captain telephoned the owner in a sleeping America, to wake him at the time of the lowest ebb of human mental agility, to seek assent to meet the cost of salvage. His sense of values, completely dulled by remoteness from the perils closing in, induced by the stability of the massive structure under his feet, and the inability of the owners to appreciate their ship's dire predicament from such a remote distance, generated no sense of reality over the ether.

The ship struck the Men Goulven rocks in raging seas on Thursday night, March 16, 1978, splitting asunder, spilling the treasure left to us by geological convulsions of a magnitude unappreciated by the mind of man, whose appearance was not to be made for millions of years. The time was so remote that mankind was not even a twinkle in the eye of simple fish life, when vast forests were being expunged in torrents of lava and molten rock. The raw material for coal, natural gas and oil was left to mature for aeons of time.

Pitting the cost of salvage, which would have saved both ship, her cargo and the spoliation of the coast of France, dear to poets, novelists, gourmets and children, against the hideous damage to this coastal jewel was a tragic event. Through various causes, all of them pronounced to be due to human failure by Courts sitting too long after the event to attract the Press, there have been many more similar disasters at sea since the *Amoco Cadiz*.

First hand descriptions of a small but powerful salvage tug snatching a large tanker from a rocky storm washed shore are as exciting as any fiction. Every second is vital and the pulling power of the tug and strength of the wire rope are as critical as the deft, quick surgery needed in heart transplants. To ask for a decision from thousands of miles away as to the amount of salvage money to part with, would be like a heart surgeon seeking instructions from his mentor miles distant on the telephone. The master on the bridge of a ship must be the decision-maker when its survival is in the balance. The British Naval officer has leave to disobey standing battle orders in the light of changed circumstances or fresh intelligence, unknown to his superiors.

The British submarine H.M.S. *Affray* met catastrophic disaster,

1) The *Amoco Cadiz*, snapped in two and disgorging her cargo of crude oil onto Brittany's holiday beaches. (Popper)

with the loss of all hands when her schnorkel pipe sheared in the early hours of the morning, the worst time for disaster to strike when mental agility is at its most sluggish. A quick decision was needed within 3 to 4 seconds as 10 tons of water per second poured through the hole. Anyone woken, even in his own bed by an alarm clock, would find a dramatic decision very difficult to make within seconds of waking. But a shipowner, with only the barest details of complex circumstances facing his ship, must have found an accurate decision impossible when remote from the drama.

With 220,000 tons of very oily light crude oil on board, and hobbled with no steering, the *Amoco Cadiz* approached disaster with adequate help at hand, but was unable to make the vital decision through a division of command that proved fatal to the ship, her cargo and the beauty of a much loved coast for many weeks.

The *Amoco Cadiz* disaster sets the scene for an appraisal of all the circumstances that face the earth's circulatory system which is menaced as never before by the steady ingestion of chemical impurities on a vast scale. A small planet cannot expect a blood change.

Seventeenth-century Great Circle Navigation gave way to twentieth-century vicious circle navigation in a rapid backward stride, when oil tankers metamorphosed from large to gigantic. At one stage in the race for greater length, breadth, depth and carrying capacity, a million tonner was mooted, with a draught of 100 feet. This was in the heady days of late 1970, and signified a jump in ten years from 100,000 tons to ten times that figure, which was too great on a number of counts. The chief one was economic viability. Today's debate is over reducing the length of tankers to make them more saleable.

The greatest misunderstanding common on the subject of ship size is in relation to their draught. Up to the end of the Second World War the deepest draught ships were battleships, with depths of thirty-three feet. Such draughts put a heavy strain on the world's hydrographers of the day, since nearly all chart marks were derived from lead and line surveys. It was not and is not appreciated that strong currents occur at varying depths in the water column, and in varying directions, and their strength and direction are not observable from the surface. Thus a line could be skilfully swung by a Panama-hatted seaman, "out East", who waited for the jolt as the lead struck the seabed, and then recorded the depth. He could not know of any aberrational currents which would bend his line into an "S" shape, giving a reading of sixty feet when there was only twenty feet under his keel. For this reason most of the charts of the world's continental shelves, such as have been surveyed at all, are at best good for rough guidance and at worst, downright misleading if not treated with caution and seamanlike suspicion. As British Admiralty Notices to Mariners put it . . . "It is becoming increasingly evident that economic pressures are causing mariners to navigate through waters of barely adequate depth, under-keel clearance being finely assessed from the charted depths and predicted tide levels. It cannot be too strongly emphasised that even charts based on modern surveys may not show all seabed obstructions, or the shoalest depths and actual tide levels may be appreciably lower than those predicted".

Captain Kokhoris, Master of the motor vessel *Agios Antonios*, writing to the Hydrographer of the British Navy from Coondapoor Harbour, in India, wrote that he had discovered, purely by chance, that there is a substantial rock in the roads outside the harbour. He gave the exact position, adding . . . "I can safely confirm the exist-ence of this rock, since my vessel is at present stranded on top of it". This could be described as a minor classic but a major one was the French passenger liner *Antilles* which grounded on an uncharted rock in the Grenadine Islands, the ship altering course to give the passengers a better view of the enchanted isle of Mustique. Disen-chantment soon followed, the grinding of metal against rock and the subsequent legal argument disclosed that the French chart of 1875 on the bridge was based on an 1861 survey, the United States chart was based on a survey in 1891, and they differed widely as to the nature of the seabed in the area. The *Antilles* had a draught of 8 metres, but any vessels when the surveys were made would have had maximum draughts of far less, and fathom marks on the charts derived from lead and line would give no indication of what was either side of the lead when it struck the bottom.

The British Hydrographer, with characteristic understatement, opined that the master had been over reliant on the charts. One could add that from 1861 to 1971, the date of the disaster, was too wide a gap to ignore, throwing caution to the winds.

The then largest single marine insurance loss in history, $14,000,000, was the brand new ore carrier *Igara* grounding on a rock near an island in the China Sea. I sent details of the event reported in *Lloyd's List*, to the President of the Directing Committee of the International Hydrographic Bureau in Monte Carlo. Admiral Ritchie replied that "if you navigate near an island you must expect other islands, albeit submerged, to be around it, and prudence demands avoidance of the whole area", especially if the survey was between 1881 and 1907 (lead and line) which the latest one did at the time of the "accident". In fact he pointed out there was entirely safe deepwater passage, not long distant to the south of the ship's terminal track.

These two disasters serve to show the vital need to use both charts and written advice in Pilot books that go with them, as guidance and not as oracular pronouncements. The commonsense advice is seldom heeded on the world's continental shelves and shallow waters, by Masters of lone wolf shipping companies, and those flying flags of convenience. Voices of people wondering "whose convenience?" are growing in frequency and strength.

A more expensive ship promoted a message from Lloyd's Sub-agents at Kota Kinabalu in February, 1974. The signal read: "Reliably informed tanker *Seaspray* with 120,000 tons of crude oil Indonesia for American destination, aground Swallow Reef. . . ." Curious to know the date of the survey on which the ship's chart was based I wrote to Admiral Ritchie in Monaco. He pointed out that the ship was aground in a dangerous area, studded with coral reefs, rocks and shoals, well known to any seaman who has ever sailed in Eastern waters. It is a vast area and he doubted it would be surveyed within the next 100 years. If the master had read his Admiralty Sailing Directions, which every prudent seaman reads in association with his charts, he would have read . . . "Palawan Passage, and the dangerous ground between it and the main route through the China

Sea . . . known to abound with dangers . . . vessels are cautioned not to attempt to pass through this area . . ." The 63,573-ton ship was grounded 20 miles inside this notorious area of unsurveyed water . . . the responsibility of no particular country to survey. I took the letter to the leading Lloyd's Underwriter of this particular Swedish Fleet, which had a hitherto excellent record. Having read it, he picked up the telephone to the owners, who opined that the ship was navigating on the "Borneo Beacon". Neither the leading Underwriter nor myself had heard of such a beacon. I contacted a previous Hydrographer of the British Navy, Admiral Sir Edmund Irving, who pointed out that it must be a short range beacon and therefore of no value at the distance of the ship to the source of the signals.

These three examples of insight into the realities of ship ground-ings are only a microcosm of the problem. The large majority of casualties reported in *Lloyd's List* sent to hydrographers all over the world, pointed the finger not at the inaccuracies of the charts made from surveys in the eighteenth and nineteenth centuries, but at the lack of ordinary good seamanship and prudence that should attend any venture into the deep oceans of the globe, or onto its continental shelves.

The difficulties facing hydrographers are that they have to work in isolation, that is, away from commerce. Their pleas for sanity at sea do not reach receptive ears outside specialist circles. They are made in the echoing halls of learned societies. Their sense of duty, long lost in commerce, is all that stands between chaos and order in the oceans and over the continental shelves of the world as they struggle for recognition of the vital nature of their work, against inertia and indifference.

Just one hundred years ago the first tanker to carry oil in bulk was built, the *Zoroaster*. She was soon followed in 1886 by the *Glückauf*, the ship which is generally accepted as the prototype of the modern oil tanker. She had a draught of 24.5 feet, and carried sail to augment her steam propulsion, which, no doubt, kept the Master and the crew alert and free from the debilitating malaise of boredom, which is the cancer of modern commercial sea life. As ships grew in size their crews became increasingly remote from the virile challenges of the wind, wave and current. Tankers no longer looked like ships and life on board became like present day commercial flying, an amalgam of fear and boredom. Their crews, no long busied with splicing anything but the mainbrace, were bereft of stimulus to muscle or brain.

From the *Glückauf* with a draught of 24 feet to 65 feet was a giant leap in less than a hundred years across uncharted seas and oceans without precedent in human history, either as to the rapidity of this carelessly undertaken step or the lethal size and nature of the cargoes to be carried. In this context it has often been claimed that two world wars, when large ships were sunk and damaged, spilling oil into the oceans, did no permanent oil pollution damage, and therefore the current rate was of lesser dimensions by several factors. This argument does not stand up to close examination, as any one with nautical experience in wartime will explain. Vessels were far smaller, including tankers, and many of them were victims of fire and explosions, so that oil was consumed and dispersed rapidly, in what are now considered small quantities.

Adding to the difficulties facing Hydrographers in modernising charts, resulting from sailing ship and oared boat surveys over one

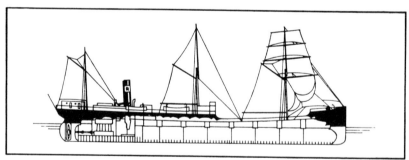

2) The *Glückauf*, built in Newcastle in 1886 by Armstrong Mitchell & Co. for the German-American Oil Co., regarded as the prototype of the modern tanker. Dimensions were 310 by 37 feet and steam engines were supplemented by sail.

hundred years ago by lead and line, was the lack of knowledge of the circumstances surrounding strandings and groundings. These circumstances are almost hidden under the suffocating blanket of "sub judice" generated by long delays in the due process of the law. By the time the truth emerges the incident is part of history and no longer attracts the attention of the Press or legislators. Such was the case with the *Torrey Canyon*. A zealous and courageous New York reporter, Richard Petrow, ferreted out the awful truth, in parallel with the Royal Institute of Navigation, too late for any impact. His book was largely ignored in England, where the catastrophe occurred. The stranding and pollution was eagerly reported by the Press at the time, but it is seldom preoccupied with history. As a British Judge observed recently, "justice delayed is justice denied".

Captain Douglas Gray, Chief Harbour Master of the Firth of Forth estuary, talking on oil pollution in his area recently said, "Some port authorities may be reluctant to prosecute, because the legal process is so prolonged that by the time damages are paid the exercise is hardly worthwhile and the amount of expert time wasted is enormous".

No blame for out-of-date charts can be laid at the doors of the world's hydrographers, whose cautions to navigators go unheeded year after year, as the average of three-and-a-half ships a day touch the ground or strand. If they had ten times the budgets allotted to them and ten times the number of survey ships, their task would still be Herculean. Approximately half of British coastal waters have never been surveyed, for example, and the surveys of the world's continental shelves are hopelessly crude for present ships' draughts. A danger that is not apparent when rapid surveys are undertaken internationally, as they were recently in the Malacca Straits, is that collisions are substituted for groundings. Instructions to navigators become so complicated in an area prone to sudden loss of vision through rain squalls that a vital turn at a buoy can be missed, leading to spectacular collisions.

It is considered too expensive for ships to use the deep Lombok Passage, suitable for big ships to avoid the over-busy Malacca Straits on the grounds that the extra fuel burned by the deviation

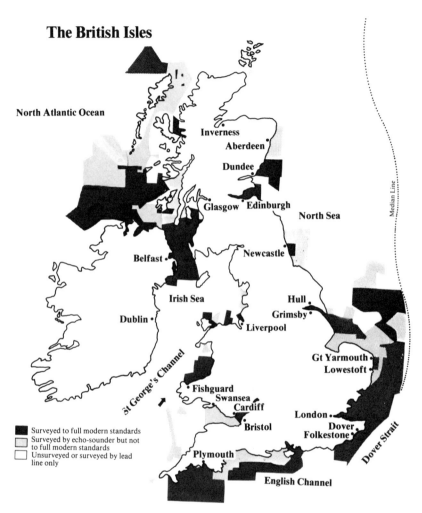

The British Isles

North Atlantic Ocean

Inverness

Aberdeen

Dundee

Glasgow Edinburgh

North Sea

Newcastle

Belfast

Irish Sea

Hull

Grimsby

Dublin

Liverpool

Gt Yarmouth
Lowestoft

Fishguard
Swansea
Cardiff

London

Bristol

Dover
Folkestone

Plymouth

English Channel

St George's Channel

Median Line

Dover Strait

Surveyed to full modern standards
Surveyed by echo-sounder but not
to full modern standards
Unsurveyed or surveyed by lead
line only

3) Seas around the British Isles charted to modern standards.

could not be justified commercially. But the New Zealand New Values Party would see the problem in a very different light.

The risk assessment is a few tons of oil against tens of thousands of tons at risk. Strandings, collisions and near misses continue in the busy Malacca Straits.

Sad victims of the rising cost of fossil fuel are the ocean liners. I enjoyed one of the last Atlantic voyages of the beautiful Italian ship *Leonardo da Vinci*. Talking to the Captain, the hero of the *Andrea Doria/Stockholm* disaster, on his bridge, I described the loss of the *Igara*, an Italian ship on her maiden voyage. He asked if there was loss of life involved in the casualty, to which I replied that no one was hurt. "Okay, what's the problem?" he said with genial finality. If the Underwriters pay without question then many accidents at sea will be repeated over and over again, and this pernicious attitude will spread. The real causes of accidents are only revealed when the public and legislators have long since forgotten the facts and the controversy surrounding it no longer attracts votes, because it is history.

The *Torrey Canyon* stranded and broke up spilling over 100,000 tons of Kuwait crude oil on March 18, 1967. By September 1968, court action instigated by the Union Oil Company in New York City was still not on the court calendar, and the British and French Governments had made little if any progress regarding blame or exoneration.

The average Maritime Court sits anything up to four years after an accident at sea. A glance at *Lloyd's List* will satisfy doubts as to such as assertion. An example was the stranding of the *London Valour* in Genoa harbour with sad loss of life on April 9, 1970. The public enquiry was started on April 19, 1972.

Studying the functions of human memory, "ego defence" and the results of sudden shock, a pioneer psychologist, Wilhelm Stern, brought the problems of hearsay, rumour and total and partial or nil recall into the psychological laboratory with startling results. In one experiment he showed his subjects pictures, and after 45 seconds asked to have them described. This process was repeated at various intervals of time, and more questioning revealed that over a period of merely weeks, errors increased dramatically. The author of "Experience and Behaviour", in describing those revealing insights into the frailties of human memory, adds that the word "see" may be taken to include being selectively blind or deaf or otherwise unperceptive to information because of contrary motivation. One would guess that such motivation would have to be caused by a dramatic "assault" and would be a progressive reversal of reality in the mind of the victim – or witness. The author heard a witness being questioned in detail, five months after the event, as to whether the gunsmoke smelled stronger in the kitchen or the living room. As Michel de Montaigne put it "a strong memory is commonly coupled with infirm judgement".

If one substitutes a young watchkeeping officer on the bridge of an ocean liner or a large heavy-laden tanker, being asked months or years after the accident "how many ships were on the radar screen and on what bearings?" he will no doubt give a crisp and clear answer, taking a leaf from Montaigne's book. In Lloyd's we speak of "radar assisted collisions", a connotation that quickly emerged from its general use at sea. "Ego defence" is one of the most potent defence mechanisms we know of, and it functions more effectively under the stress of Courts of Law seeking for guilt or innocence than elsewhere. The *Torrey Canyon* Court of Enquiry in Genoa, described in the *Journal of the Royal Institute of Navigation*, brings the point out vividly, that a man can convince himself that an event he describes is accurate, when the reverse is true. Her Captain was asked "did you have the best ship in the world?" On this question and his answer to it devolved the whole case of the shipowner's involvement in liability. The questioner was patently more alert than the mentally exhausted Captain Rugiati, who had had no shore leave for an incredible twelve months. His affirmative answer exonerated the owners from all blame. The real governing facts, so ably extracted by Richard Petrow and members of the Royal Institute of Navigation, became irrelevant and obscured: fuses blowing in the remotely-controlled steering system, no charts or Admiralty Pilot book of the area where the ship stranded, master and chief officer at odds with one another and so on.

A weak-willed, shocked or tired mind will always buckle under a strong-willed vigorous Attorney.

John Carrothers, writing in the U.S. Naval Institute's *Proceedings* fifteen years after the disastrous *Andrea Doria* and *Stockholm* collision, produced ample proof that if the evidence of one side in the Court hearing was to be believed, the *Stockholm* would have had to execute an "S" shaped manoeuvre at a speed exceeding 2,500 miles an hour, to gain the position she claimed to be in! One year after the collision, the Marine Editor of the *New York Times*, George Horne, referred to the word "accident", so freely used in collisions at sea, and strandings and groundings. The word, he said, has inherent connotations of *unforeseeable* and *unavoidable*. Reading the evidence produced by careful U.S. Naval procedures, sifting through masses of computer print-outs and so on, the word "accident" becomes less and less relevant.

Ordinary prudence and good seamanships were totally ignored by both ships. This assertion is made in the Royal Institute of Navigation's *Journal*. It concluded from the stated evidence that the *Andrea Doria* was improperly ballasted at the time of impact. Her ballast tanks had largely been emptied on the side presented to the *Stockholm*, since pumping out oil contaminated water was prohibited in New York Harbour, and quicker refuelling would result from empty ballast tanks. She was thus unable to stay upright after the crash.

As Mr. Carrothers put it "for those whose prime interest in accident cases is safety and education, there is no satisfaction in pointing the finger of guilt. Yet facts are facts, and they have an eloquence of their own. Accidents don't just happen; they are caused. By examining the causes, valuable lessons can always be learned, by and for the men who are, and will be, in charge of the watch on the bridges of ships." It is all too easy to demonstrate that the contrary is the case, all over the globe. Such safe advice struck few of the targets that this writer aimed to hit, since few watchkeeping officers on tankers and fewer ship operators are members of the U.S. Naval Institute which published the article.

Thus the people who know cannot reach those who should know, and this lamentable state of affairs is compounded by the archaic custom of muzzling serving officers speaking in public.

When the *Torrey Canyon* struck the Seven Stones rocks, she had no Admiralty Pilot book of the area, which must be used in conjunction with any Admiralty chart. Some years ago I opened a speech in Washington, written at twelve hours' notice, with the words "no one in this audience would like to take off from Dulles Airport knowing that the navigator's air map was made before the Wright Brothers became airborne. Ships traversing the world's continental shelves are navigating with charts that in some cases have not been corrected, or even surveyed by lead and line or single line echo sounders, since the days of steam, if not sail."

The problem is made worse by other factors. The fathom, as a measure, is elastic, being a measure of outstretched arms' lengths, varying between Spain, France and Britain as to measurement when the charts were first made. Further, neither spring nor neap tides nor wave action were taken into account by early chart makers. Nor was the fact that lead sinkers meeting ooze just "went on down" giving false depth readings. Despite these considerations, the past five years have demonstrated that few groundings and strandings have been caused by antique charts.

The well publicised voyage of the specially adapted tanker *Manhattan* across the top of Canada, to demonstrate that oil could be transported on the hazardous route is a case in point. The ship missed a "pengo" rock pinnacle spotted by an ice breaker by a few feet, but this was not given wide publicity. For a sound decision as to the feasibility of commercial submarine tankers in these hostile waters one has only to read the reports of the U.S. Navy submarine *Nautilus* under the polar ice, with only a few feet of clearance at top and bottom, albeit that she was bristling with all manner of omnidirectional sensing devices.

The penultimate voyage of the ferry from St. John's, Newfoundland to Goose Bay, Labrador, and back, yielded an intriguing insight into the state of hydrographic charts in the area. At a placid stage in the unusually calm voyage a fellow passenger, who knew the coast from many years of fishing it, became very excited, exclaiming that the ship was to go through the "Indian Tickle" for the first time. Intrigued I asked what this meant, to be told that a "tickle" was a shallow passage between island and mainland that could only be used safely in calm, clear weather. I sought admission to the bridge to look at the First Officer's planned route on the chart, and turning it over, found that the survey of the whole area was made in 1885. The *William Carson* sank in mysterious circumstances in the open sea on her next spring voyage.

In late 1978 I was sitting in a hotel room in Los Angeles with a number of fellow delegates at an Oceanographic Conference, five of whom had participated actively in the recovery of the H-bomb, accidentally dropped off Palomares on the Spanish Mediterranean coast. The pilot of the submersible *Alvin* described how the track made by the bomb over a mud slope had been spotted, leading to its discovery. Knowing that the most up-to-date chart during the search was Spanish, *c*. 1865, I asked if it was a result of luck, or of a long methodical search, and the answer was "luck". It is a widely held popular misconception that the charts of even the world's continental shelves are checked and rechecked at regular intervals. A major part of them have never been surveyed at all, and those areas surveyed are so poorly and inaccurately marked from lead and line surveys, as to be at best, misleading, and at worst dangerously inaccurate.

Before leaving the subject of inadequate ocean mapping for the broader issues that lead to pollution of the ocean, an insurance enquiry a few years ago on a large commercial submarine, the *Auguste Piccard*, is another illustration of the point. Tourist interests in California sent glossy brochures to their Lloyd's Brokers depicting beautiful girls peering at exotic fish in the Seychelles "underwater paradise", with a handsome smartly dressed Captain in white peaked cap at the controls. A glance at the chart of the whole area told one that it was largely unsurveyed, and the facilities for ordinary running repairs and maintenance of the submarine to carry 40 passengers was non-existent in the only available small port. An oceanographer friend, well versed in the practicalities of undersea work, put the matter in his fractured English in this way "Zis submarine is equipped with saddle tanks, one on each side. If ze coral punctures one of zeze – ze submarine will be UPSIDEDOWN".

The problem of buying insurance on 40 expensive American ladies, at a minimum of $1,000,000 each, in one small space in a remote part of the world, proved too exotic for London Underwriters, and the venture died. It left a vivid picture of a large submarine with 40 ladies hanging upside down, being peered at by curious tropical fish. But the saving of many lives dominates this picture.

Regulation of idiocy on the surface is quite another story. If "good example'" governed losses of men and ships at sea there would be a falling graph of incidents. Instead, it is on a steeply rising one. In 1972 a headline in *Lloyd's List* read: "Record tonnage losses in 1971. The highest since World War II". The same headline appeared in early 1979, describing the record million tons lost in 1978. The good example is provided by the large oil companies who run great fleets of tankers. They provide tough training programmes for officers and crew, inert gas systems to lessen the risk of explosion in half emptied tanks, and in general have a tight grip on safety. Like the wisdom and experience of hydrographers, these laudable procedures go unheard and unsung outside the confines of the large companies, and are thus not followed by those who cause most of the maritime oil and chemical pollution.

Putting the gigantic tasks facing European survey work into present day context is all too easy, but sad to say the examples come from publications with relatively small spheres of influence. Rear Admiral David Haslam, Hydrographer of the Royal Navy, spoke his usual trenchant, pithy and timely advice to the Royal Institute of Navigation at a meeting in Warsash (Warsash, Southampton) reported in the Institute's *Journal*. He describes vividly the metamorphosis from crude lead and line surveys to sophisticated side-scan sonars towed astern by the survey ships under his command. He goes on "we now know that there are some 16,000 wrecks, or parts of wrecks, somewhere within our coastal waters. We do not know the exact position of more than 12,500, or the exact depth over some 14,000 of such wrecks. The position may be wildly in error". Semi and slightly buoyant wrecks frequently move many miles from where they sank, and wrecks are covered and uncovered by sand waves. "The value of side-scan surveys carried out by H.M.S. *Bulldog* can be illustrated by the work in 1977, in a 200-square-mile area of the Dover Strait, between the coast from Dover to Dungeness, and the Varne Bank; the ship was given 169 wrecks found in this small but busy area during the 1960 survey, using the best means then available. She found over 500 contacts and, although many proved to be negligible irregularities of the sea bed, over 60 previously unknown wrecks were found, including 12 with less than 23 metres (76 feet) of water over them." Admiral Haslam points out that examination of the seabed by side-scan sonar is a slow business, at less than 6 knots over the ground, to avoid missing a rock pinnacle or a ship's mast as it flashes past.

This insight into the mammoth task faced by this dedicated service harassed by changes of Government, throwing up Ministers with minimal comprehension of the nature and importance of the hydrographer's work, must be seen in the context of giant tankers with depths of up to 95 feet, like the ultra large crude carrier *Atlantic*. Assumptions are made, and the most common one in seafaring today is that nautical charts are as accurate as ordnance surveys or air maps. One must explode such dangerous fallacies by again quoting the hydrographer . . . "For my first survey in 1944 we still used the hand-leadline, though not oarsmen, as in the early surveys. Our soundings covered only the few square centimetres actually struck by the lead and objects a foot away from each cast remained undetected". It is appreciated by very few people, hydrographers and skilled yachtsmen among them, that nautical charts are advisory and not delphic. They must be interpreted and if your keel stretches 70 feet into the water, you must use considerable insight.

Life at sea has traditionally been an adventure, pitting one's wits against the treachery of currents, winds and waves. This does not apply to large flat bottomed tankers of over 50,000 tons or so. In the past merchant and naval sailing ships used masts as pendulums, and the power of wind, and wave, to weave a path through the turmoil of the seas with skill, sliding and gliding to gain momentum through the water. Big ships fight the ocean head on, punching into the weather with the pugnacity of a bulldozer. This is on the mistaken notion that money is saved by travelling in a straight line, and this is another subject which will take its place later in this book.

If some computer theoreticians had their way, ships would go to sea remotely controlled from the land. This theory already has a glimmer of practice around it, and a Japanese shipbuilder recently described a 214-metre (702-foot) ship with a "crew" of only seven officers and Deck Petty Officer and a steward. Special care was taken in the study regarding the mental health of the crew! A few years ago a system was mooted to monitor ships at sea from a central point ashore. Thus a Master would receive a message like "Don't look now, but your forepeak is on fire". Or "The hydraulics on your steering engine are about to collapse" (as they did in the *Amoco Cadiz*, bringing her into intimate and terminal contact with the French coast). The idea never took off for the simple reason that shipowners were not interested in investing large sums in an unproven system. Thus another brave project died, through lack of knowledge of the nuts and bolts of ship profitability.

It is a popular myth that new safety devices such as this will persuade insurance Underwriters to concede lower premiums if they are carried. In fact the insurance industry requires proof of success of any system over a long period before conceding premium reductions. The introduction of radar to commercial shipping led to pleas for premium reductions from shipowners fitting the "safety device" in their ships. Marine insurers insisted on eating the pudding before proving it, and thus "radar assisted collisions" was coined.

So long as a measure of control is to prevail at sea, men and women will have to man ships. As time passes, operations become more dehumanised however and as ship casualties increase, the attractions of a seafaring life tend to wane. Against this background there is a chronic shortage of ship's officers, captains and crew. A British ship's Master asks the question "are we producing mere ship drivers, not sea officers?" If little skill is required in large oil carrying ships, they become mere "pipelines", and what man can be persuaded that this has any attraction as a way of life . . . ?

The smaller shipowners cannot afford the luxuries of exhaustive training programmes and competition becomes the enemy of safety, increasing as demand for ships wanes, making an insurance recovery an attractive proposition on a loss making ship. One can speculate on the deliberate scuttling of the *Christos Bitas* in mid-October 1978, and what pressures were exerted from what directions upon whom. This could be termed idle speculation if put before the Marine Insurance Community, who tend to avoid brooding on past history and look to the future with pens poised ready to increase premiums when their records dictate that a whole class of business requires corrective treatment.

4) Oil from *Christos Bitas* **is pumped into another tanker alongside before the ship was scuttled in the mid-Atlantic. (BP)**

Manning standards have declined sharply in the past ten years, in the same ratio as accidents at sea have increased. The decline is due to identifiable causes, and it is an advantage to have served in ocean going ships to grasp the most telling ones. In the journal of Captain Woodes Rogers of a long sea voyage at the beginning of 1698 there is a vivid description of two of His Majesty's ships in company in boisterous seas bordering the Bay of Biscay. One Captain signals the other to come aboard for a glass of Madeira wine at 11 o'clock, and receives a quick assent. The guest climbs down his gangway and steps into his gig, which is bobbing up and down like a piece of cork, as if it were in a flat calm. His boat's crew pull with consummate skill towards the other ship's gangway, using every wave to hasten the passage, and the Captain jumps onto the gangway with balletic grace, and after the party is over, the process is repeated. As the editor pointed out in a recent shortened version of the journal, nowadays the boat's crew would be awarded gold watches for such demonstrations of skill and bravery. A wry comment on the sense of duty can be seen in the Nelson Room at Lloyd's where Nelson's famous message to the Fleet at Trafalgar "England expects that every man will do his duty" is depicted in the flag hoist on the wall. There was no single hoist for the word "duty", and it had to be spelled in letters. The notion of duty was so ingrained in British seamen at the time that the word was superfluous in the Signal Book.

While it is obvious that life at sea was appallingly tough in those days, it is clear that in all the days of sail there was a pride and exhilaration in demonstrating skills, and rivalry between ships, both military and commercial. Boredom was a luxury almost unknown. This was the case in the ships in which I served during the Second World War, up to 1946. All manner of things were made in the spare time allowed by fair weather and "make and mend" spells . . . as in previous days sailors had made wool pictures, ships in bottles, knitting, ship models, and sing songs were being held, and a camaraderie emerged in every ship. Today this is rare, one fine if rare example to follow is the salvage tug firm L. Smit and Company, who favour the idea of ships' crews all coming from the same town or village. They thus know each other and insights develop that are vital in a crisis.

Take the collision of two 326,000 dead weight ton tankers, *Venoil* and *Venpet*, on December 16, 1977 off the Cape of Good Hope. Results of the Court's finding were examined by a retired U.S. Coast Guard Captain a year after the event. One can feel confident that the result of the hearings held by the Liberian Court sitting in the United States in February, 1978 did not excite comment from either the world's daily Press, or from legislators. This is what was disclosed. Some thirty one thousand tons of crude and bunker oil were released into the sea, and two lives were lost. Imagine a transatlantic jet aircraft with no formalised flight deck procedures, or team training even for normal flight aside from emergencies. But such was the case with both ships.

The *Venoil*'s Master had been on board less than a month and as Captain, only two weeks at the time of the accident. Despite the

5) The Liberian-flag tanker *Venoil* ablaze off Cape St. Francis near Port Elizabeth, South Africa, December 1977. (Associated Press)

Venpet's Master having been on board for two years, there was no formalised bridge team training in that ship, either. The former ship's radar, Decca Navigator and bridge watch officers were all new to the Captain. There they were approaching each other at full economical speed, about 14 knots through fog. With the radar of one of them some 15 degrees out of calibration (a difference of four miles in accuracy), it was an "accident waiting to happen". Both ships carried radio telephones, but neither ship used them as they closed in at a combined speed of nearly 30 knots in poor visibility. Vessels of this size would need 15 minutes or two miles for a crash stop when fully laden. In addition to this chain of disaster, there was no effective bridge lookout on either vessel during the approach at speed in fog, nor was there a lookout on the bows, several football pitch lengths from the bridge. Just add that the *Venpet* Ship's time was eight or nine minutes slow and you have a crescendo of folly difficult to believe but tragically true.

The fact that many of the circumstances described were in blatant breach of the basic provisions of the International Regulations for Prevention of Collisions at sea, proves beyond doubt that neither national nor international regulations can regulate a total disregard for common sense seamanship. This contention is strengthened when one contemplates the accepted originator of a celebrated major marine oil spill, the *Torrey Canyon*. The circumstances of the disaster bear retelling when set down beside those of the *Venoil* and *Venpet*.

Captain Rugiati, the Master of the *Torrey Canyon*, had been at sea for a year without shore leave. This in itself can either mean dedication to his job, or to a psychiatrist alienation, depending on whether the reader is thoughtful or cynical. But the fact that the other lamentable circumstances leading to the catastrophe were not taken up at the time, meant that these vital lessons went unlearnt. Twelve years later they are considered as history and in no corridors of power are they discussed as sources of material for legislation.

To begin with, little but local controversy was generated over the explosive pollution of Bantry Bay by the *Betelgeuse*, with regard to the method of discharging her cargo. Her French owners, when asked why an inert gas system was not fitted to the ship (not necessarily germane to the cause of the explosion), are quoted as saying, "it was not mandatory in that class of ship". In July 1980 the Irish government published a report on the *Betelgeuse* explosion which squarely indicted the operating companies for the dangerous condition of the ship. Yet the dangers, inherent in an increasingly rich mixture of air with volatile gases, led to another explosion halfway across the world in Manila Bay on November 8, 1978 when the *Feoso Sun* disintegrated taking 30 lives through a rapid and lethal chain of events. The facts that one ship exploded in an area of sparse population, albeit taking 50 lives, and the other in a heavily populated area taking 30 lives was not a matter of planning, since the risks of explosion had evidently been discounted by the parties concerned. If they had occurred in New York Harbour or at Canvey Island the tragedy would have been magnified a hundred or a thousand fold, and it is pure luck that this has not occurred.

The development of larger and larger ships being controlled by fewer and fewer men must be seen in the context of more and more new ports being developed, remote from towns and cities, so that shore leave is truncated by the length of time needed to reach the nearest town and return in time for the quick turn around required by the owners or charterers. One strong appeal of seafaring has always centred round the attractions of shore leave and more and more men and women will leave seafaring for want of this attraction and stimulus. Long periods between ports is yet another factor that leads to boredom and to broken marriages, described as the "intermittent husband syndrome" by a consultant psychiatrist in Aberdeen, who treats oil rig workers' wives, deprived of their husbands' company over long periods.

An interesting exercise was undertaken by the Netherlands Maritime Institute, concerning the stranding of the 210,000-ton tanker, *Metula*, using just the data available at the time that the ship struck the Satellite Patch at full speed. Their conclusion was that the casualty, which excited such a head of steam in Washington circles, was caused by "poor ship and shore based planning contributing significantly to the grounding". The details of the cause of this major pollution are, if they were ever discovered by examining the Liberian

6) The *Venpet* with its distinctive skeleton bridge, with flames leaping from the collision point with the *Venoil*. (Associated Press)

Court of Enquiry's findings, lost to public notice, mainly because they were published long after the gloss of newsworthiness of the story ceased to shine.

If one translates these few examples into aviation terms, there would be spectacular crashes in mid-air all over the world, and the demise of commercial flying. The big tanker battalions only share in the responsibility for such chaos to the extent that too many of them charter ships which their experience tells them are well below their own self-imposed safety manning and planning standards. The carefully documented state on board the *Torrey Canyon* when she struck the rocks, if translated to aviation language would have led to a disaster emulating in horror the carnage of the two jumbo jets colliding in the Canary Islands.

It is a strange metamorphosis that a maritime nation such as Great Britain should accept the immediacy of disaster reports involving aircraft and reject it when it involves ships and the defilement of beautiful coastal areas. There are a number of reasons for this fundamental change. The main reason is that accidents involving ships flying flags of convenience mean that court actions are held in countries other than that where the accident occurred, often months after the event, as it did with the *Torrey Canyon*. Delay in Maritime Court hearings must in part be caused by the vastly increasing legal activity derived from the steady growth in oil spillages, which not only clog beaches, but also benches. To keep pace with major casualties involving serious pollution is a full time job, but to follow up the root causes is virtually impossible.

One of the quickest growing industries was the naming of rocks and reefs after the ships that foundered on them, but that pace has been far outstripped by spillages. They are widespread, and no respecters of climate, beauty of coastline, or marine life, including birds and small animals. In February, 1979 the Russian *Antonio Gramsci* ran aground off Ventspils, spilling 6,000 tonnes of oil making a slick seven nautical miles by 13, threatening the Finnish South West Archipelago with delayed shock. The oil has been held back by a 20-mile ice barrier . . . but when that melts, the damage will be widespread.

It is inarguable that the major oil companies, managing large fleets of oil tankers, have highly effective training programmes and thoroughly seamanlike practices, including regular inspection of ships and equipment. They frequently proclaim this at conferences on ship safety, and no-one can argue against their well upheld safety records. The tendency has been and remains, to opine that in their capable hands there is no cause for the world to excite itself on the subject of pollution of the oceans. They relate how by its nature heavy crude oil tends to sink, and lighter oils or spirits create only "flash" damage, the spillage quickly evaporating. This argument is attractive to harassed legislators and music to those owners who consistently disregard safe practices in loading and unloading tankers, and by cutting corners, ignoring safe practices at sea.

It is considered acceptable for tanker owners who charter ships which subsequently cause pollution to disclaim any responsibility, on the grounds that they cannot control the ship's behaviour which is not under their management or direct control. But this tenet weakens when compared with aviation practice. Airlines using aeroplanes to fulfil schedules, due to temporary shortages of their own aircraft, insist on their own standards of safety as to the state of the aircraft, and they provide their own crews on commercial airlines of any significant size albeit elbowed by legislation, made effective by alert-minded legislators all over the world. No such alert-minded braking mechanisms exist to regulate the chaos in the world's oceans and harbours today.

There is no Government or Agency anywhere, sufficiently far seeing or powerful to stop outright the explosions, fires, groundings and strandings that are fouling our planet and sentencing our great-grandchildren to death in a cold climate. There is no cogent challenge to the insanity ruling over the carriage of precious and dangerous substances across the face of the earth, and no powerful lobby, as there is with nuclear power or aviation, to make mankind face his future with any degree of confidence. The ordinary person is bemused by conflicting "expert" evidence on changing climate, shortage of fossil fuels, the longevity of oil spilled in sea water and the waxing or dwindling world stocks of edible fish.

Where are we to look for guidance? The answer seems to be in practical common sense and the backing of sound case histories, produced sufficiently early to give real impact to the argument. This is the object of this book. The knowledge and research of the world's hydrographers, the evidence of case histories, emerging many months after severe casualties at sea, of a damning nature to owner, charterer or deck officers, and attacks on deliberate delays in court hearings are the only effective weapons left to the ultimate victims, you and I, and our children's children.

There is no international weekly newsletter reporting successful prosecutions following maritime court cases involving blame, and paucity of material is the simple reason. The flow of such information is glacial in its slowness and one has to be sharp-eyed to find articles in technical magazines and books describing the deliberations of maritime courts, written by zealous reporters for audiences that are too thin to make their efforts rewarding. Without immediacy and sensational disclosures to feed the daily Press and television screens, the world is bored and unreceptive.

It should not be thought that spilt fossil fuels are the only cause for alarm. In 1978, 270 containers, standard cargo boxes, were tipped into the traffic lanes of world shipping, and in the context of the container being the most anonymous cargo receptacle ever carried, this is an unknown danger of fearsome proportions. The information is published on a daily basis in *Lloyd's List* and other publications, but has not hitherto been quantified in any journal.

The nature of the cargo carried in these large boxes, which present seductively squared surfaces to the assaults of aggressive ocean waves, is unknown in the vast majority of ocean passages made. The reports in *Lloyd's List* are merely those containers *sighted*, three reported adrift off the East coast of the United States the day I wrote these lines, and those occasionally reported lost by the container-carrying ships themselves. The figure would be fearsome indeed if all losses were reported and quantified. The nature and quantity of objects dropped into the oceans will be the subject of a later chapter.

Captain Ralph Maybourn, Director of British Petroleum's Tanker Fleet said in March 1979 . . . "Although tankers were usually the best run and equipped ships at sea, standards are being affected by the serious recession in the shipping industry. The tanker industry has been in recession for the past five years and will remain in recession for perhaps another five. Most owners are now in a serious financial condition and many are going bankrupt. The effect of this may well be that standards fall before profits return. There is a worldwide shortage of properly trained and experienced crews, and the operational standards of tankers vary according to owners." Mr. Maybourn advises the U.K. Government's Pollution Control Unit, and is a respected member of the British marine community.

Harking back to the opening page of this book, it would be inconceivable for a group of ship's captains and deck officers to lobby their Government to improve ship safety or arrest pollution today. The noises made by unions are recorded in the minutes of meetings that remain remote from the world's Presses and other means of broadcasting grievances. Pollution studies and the discussion of ship manning standards come and go with the frequency and incandescence of St. Elmo's Fire. A study of the deliberations of conferences on the subjects of tanker construction, operation and destruction over the past fifteen years or so, is a depressing exercise, when read in conjunction with the rising graphs of disasters and spillages at sea over the same period. Nothing has changed except the frequency of strandings, groundings, explosions and collisions, which are increasing every year in orders of magnitude, as recognition dawns on the world that fossil fuel is as finite as the sudden demise of tropical rain forests in the period after the Continents split from the vast mass of Gondwanaland millions of years ago.

Man's recorded history passes with the speed of a camera shutter in the face of such majestic geological movements, and his preoccupation with speed is ironic by comparison, producing by-products that were never intended under nature's carefully balanced laws.

Before being accused of impractical meandering by the stern demands of commerce, the argument will return to hard present day realities. The repetition of daily accidents at sea yields little in terms of impact, due to an *embarras de richesses* as well as to the boredom of remoteness from one's front room. More impact can be gained from the successful venture by The Center for Short-Lived Phenomena, a weekly *Oil Spill Intelligence Report*. This comprehensive, unemotional and accurate newsletter gives one a unique ringside seat on the alarming waste of fuels and lubricants during the dawning era of cognisance of the coming shortages, which is going to affect the politics and economies of every community, country and nation on earth. The need for such a synthesised publication has existed for years, and it complements the daily reports in *Lloyd's List*.

In the opinion of two distinguished authorities in the United States, one Naval and the other civilian, there is a need for an *Amoco Cadiz* sized pollution on the shores of North America to alert legislators to the necessity of effective legislation to stop the lethal wastage of oil. One was Admiral Harley Nygren of the National Oceanic and Atmospheric Administration in Washington, and the other, Art McKenzie, the Director of the U.S. Tanker Advisory Center, Inc, and they are not alone in this view. Public ignorance of the fearful

trends is lamentably widespread and this also applies to governments. Whenever a large coastal spillage occurs, Congressmen,
Members of Parliament and Deputies become instant experts vehe-
mently denouncing idiocy that resulted in the pollution in their
constituents' area, and after a discharge of outraged commonsense
placid calm returns and all is forgotten until the next stylised ritual.

The most frustrated brotherhood, to which Admiral Nygren
belongs, is that of hydrographers, who are the finest seamen in the
world and have to witness such imbecility on their doorsteps. I have
been in constant correspondence for a number of years with the
Head of the Directing Committee at the International Hydrographic
Centre in Monaco, Admiral Steve Ritchie. In every serious case of
groundings of ships reported in *Lloyd's List* each day, he and his staff
have been able to reject the notion that out-of-date surveys were the
cause. In one case a large tanker under impeccable ownership found
itself in "foul ground" in the Western China Sea, an area where no
ship of whatever size is safe. It was found that the ship was navigating on a short-range beacon too far distant for safe navigation and a
doubtful method of safely navigating one of the largest mobile
objects every built.

In 1971, the then hydrographer of the Navy, Rear Admiral Hall,
wrote in *Admiralty Notices to Mariners*, "It is becoming increasingly
evident that economic pressures are causing mariners to navigate
through waters of barely adequate depth . . . it cannot be too
strongly emphasised that even charts based on modern surveys may
not show all sea bed obstructions or the shoalest depths and actual
tide levels may be appreciably lower than those predicted." This
admonishment which was aimed at shipowners using continental
shelf routes fell on blind eyes and deaf ears, as a glance at *Lloyd's List*
daily casualties will demonstrate all too clearly. Another hydrographic admonishment, blithely ignored, is that charts must be
"interpreted" and not read as delphic oracles whose accuracy is not
open to question. Thus with the ore-carrier *Igara* the International
Hydrographer, Admiral Ritchie, stated that in ill surveyed areas,
such as obtain in Far Eastern seas, if a vessel sails near an island, the
master must assume that there are other "islands" in the area which

are beneath the surface. In fact, the owners collected a total loss on the vessel, the expensive afterpart being cunningly salvaged by the expert use of explosives, and a new bow fitted, to sail the seas again to the great satisfaction of the owners and the frustration and discomfiture of her insurers.

Any year will do, to demonstrate the increase in ship losses and wastage of fuels. Take 1974, the then worst settlement in history with Lloyd's Intelligence Services reporting 681,706 gross tons lost, worth £117,060,516. Since then a host of proposals have been mooted, by Governments, by International Maritime Consultancy Organisations and by individuals defending their constituents, as with the Member of Parliament for that part of the beautiful Welsh coast, when the *Christos Bitas* endeavoured to sail through it. An interesting facet of this piece of folly was the blanket of silence imposed by the then officials of the U.K. Department of Trade. All too frequently the reasons for the initial spillage are outshone by the salvage story and precious lessons lost, by the subsequent salvage operations, in this case brushing 2,420 tons of Iranian crude oil under the carpet, ignoring the corpses of over 2,000 birds and an indeterminate count of fauna. The true cause of the accident, attributed by a widely experienced tanker captain to a serious navigational error being the only possible cause of being so far off course in near perfect conditions, has to date not been divulged, whilst the world waits for the result of an enquiry under the Merchant Shipping Acts, which will be published long after interest has died.

Most catastrophes at sea end in this inconclusive way, and by the time the truth emerges through successful sleuthing by zealous journalists, it is of no news value.

The one time Australian hydrographer, Commodore Tony Cooper, tells of wartime survey work in the Philippines, when his ship was temporarily in harbour. The Master of an American Liberty ship asked to come aboard, bringing a wooden box with him. From the box he produced a sextant, and asked the hydrographer how it worked. This story opens up a problem of vast proportions.

There is another story of Henry Kaiser, the builder of hundreds of "utility" ships, Liberties, Victories, "T2" tankers and vessels of superior build, "C1's" and "2's" and "3's" that sped down the ways of American shipyards to keep pace with the depredations of U-boat wolf-packs. Kaiser is reported to have invited the wife of a Senator to launch one of his ships, handing her a bottle of Californian champagne on the end of a cord. To her enquiry "Where is the ship?" he replied "Lady. Swing the bottle and the ship'll be there." Now ships being flung into the oceans at such a rate had to make do with "instant captains". This being in the days of large convoys the war-built sheep could rely on experienced Naval officers to shepherd them in convoy, without their having to lean on navigational aids with any great weight.

The gallantry displayed by the crews manning these rapidly built vessels is legendary, and a cause for pride on both sides of the Atlantic. What occurred when swords were turned into plough-shares however is a tale yet untold. Many captains, mates and second and third officers were put on the beach until rescue came from the U.S. Government releasing war-built ships to commerce on preferential terms. Massive response came from the United States shipping community and the term "dual valuation" was on the lips of insurance Brokers and Underwriters in the world's Marine Markets. A ship could be purchased for $500,000 and was promptly and legally insured for three times that sum, to cover the cost of repairs which rose almost daily, and to prevent the ship from becoming a "Constructive Total Loss" every time it suffered slight damage, when the cost of repairs would exceed the value for which a new ship could be purchased from the Government. The accident record of these ships, frequently in the hands of officers with only war-time service, uncluttered by training in navigation above the most cursory kind demanded by convoy work, was fearsome.

As commercial shipping found its feet, the war-built vessels began to show their age, and the United States Government relaxed the requirements to favour only the U.S. flag in tonnage disposals. Thus was born the Flag of Convenience, and ships' captains sprang up all over the globe and the rot set in, where it has flourished ever since. At the time, marine technology, as a braking mechanism, was said to be "low, man, on the totem pole; it doesn't have the votes" and practical seamanship became archaic, like steam trains.

2. The "Lutine" Bell

Ten years ago in the small Board Room of an oceanographic ship owner in Bethesda, near Washington D.C., the workings of marine insurance were being dismantled and reassembled to benefit a consultant who had been called in, "to examine the insurance programme". The consultant had been through all the papers to justify his fees, concerning the past year's operations of the company all over the world, insured at Lloyd's and elsewhere among London based insurance companies. He waded in with objections to the inclusion of " . . . pirates, rovers, thieves . . . letters of mart and countermart, surprisals . . . " as being archaic wording, not germane to the risks of today and thus assuming that he had made a bull point. It had to be explained that the words on the "Lloyd's of London" policies had been tested in every Court in the world, over three centuries, and that other words stuck on supplanted them where present-day needs demanded. To remove the basic policy would be like the removal of one's skeleton to promote a more supple body. Explaining this, without loss of face to a consultant floundering in unfamiliar maritime waters, took all the diplomacy available from experience as a marine insurance Broker at Lloyd's. But happily it worked and no damage was done.

A look at how Lloyd's functions should give an insight into its role in the prevention or cure of pollution of our oceans and rivers. Some time before 1689, a Mr. Edward Lloyd did something that Americans find beyond belief for an Englishman to achieve: he made good coffee. This gift, alien to the true Briton, led to his Coffee House becoming popular through a wide spectrum of citizens around the Tower Street area of the City of London. Among these were bankers, shipowners and owner-captains of ships trading abroad. Confidence grew between them, as risks were shared more widely and shipowners suffering disaster at sea were quickly re-imbursed and soon, at Christmas-time in 1691, Lloyd's moved to Lombard Street. This street is still the heart of London banking circles, which are not as heartless as might be supposed; by this time a formidable intelligence network existed to keep Underwriters informed of events abroad that could mean profit or loss, for want of quick reactions over disposal of perishable or easily pilferable goods, for instance, and penetration of "mysterious disappearances".

The "growth" of Lloyd's of London is nowadays a misnomer, since growth implies more and more rapid metamorphosis, ending in the terminal descent of profitability graphs. Lloyd's slowly matured, learning by its mistakes and unhurried by the pressures of quick profits which step on the heels of quick losses, and as it grew in size, so it widened in knowledge and experience, increasingly put to use. This is the great strength of this institution. It is necessary to explain in better detail the nature of the place and its people. It is a popular misconception that Lloyd's has a corporate voice and acts corporately. In fact it is a market, and brokers shop for insurance there, with the Underwriters acting "each for himself and not one for the other". They do this in one large room, where they sit in "boxes" made from mahogany, some of them still writing risks with quill pens. There are of course braking mechanisms and regulatory committees as there are in any sound corporation, but the Committee and the Chairman seldom if ever interfere with the day-to-day affairs of the Underwriters.

To illustrate the nature of this slow expansion, Membership of Lloyd's was 2,000 in 1940 and 15,000 in 1978. Premium income, unrelated to losses, was £100 million in 1945, increasing to over ten times this figure in 1974. Detractors tend to attack the system as monopolistic and worse, a rich man's Club. Metamorphosis, in the real democratic sense of the "power of the people" cannot be monopolistic, since it acts by the common will, in the case of Lloyd's to provide a market for insurance. No one is obliged to shop there, but if it provides uniquely sound security, and a healthy competitive democratic climate, it offers a unique service to the Community.

There are many true stories, enough to provide Samuel Smiles with a second volume of his Victorian eulogy of men and women from humble beginnings reaching the top echelons through real ability, innovation or flair. There is no premium on wealth or influence to stop ability from flowering in Lloyd's that has been observable over nearly forty years of daily attendance in the Underwriting Room.

Any market worth its salt waxes and wanes in strength, and we talk of an Underwriters' Market and a Brokers' Market. Catastrophes seem to occur in cycles, and as a cycle of few catastrophes continues, other markets in other countries and areas of the world step in and provide competition, that in normal commercial climates are healthy. But when the notion that insurance is a field of certain profit begins to be accepted, as it does, from time to time, danger looms for all. A catastrophe such as the San Francisco earthquake in 1906 illuminates the strength of Lloyd's, and refutes the accusation of monopolistic practices. Then Lloyd's Underwriters paid the victims quickly and in full. Many competitors in the United States and elsewhere did not.

As Antonio says, in Shakespeare's *Merchant of Venice*:

"I thank my fortune for it, my ventures are not in one bottom trusted, nor to one place; nor is my whole estate upon the fortune of this present year."

Spreading risks is the soundest of commercial concepts started by primitive man with food caches in widely dispersed caves. A weak market, when competition comes from zealous newcomers to the field such as banks and financiers means that too many high risks are polarized into too few areas of underwriting. Sanity returns finally for those with security and resilience sound enough to face another cycle, offering continuity of insurance cover which is a necessity for any sound business house.

A number of fields of marine and other kinds of insurance have been pioneered at Lloyd's. It should be said however that despite the allusion to the entrance of banking into the fray when times are good, there are records from 1335 of Francesco di Marco, Merchant of Prato, just north of Florence, proving the early familiarity of banks with marine insurance. It was common for such merchants to take out insurance policies, backed by banks, against the depredations of storm and piracy.

One of the fields that required imagination and a high degree of sound judgement, with little time to make vital decisions, was the insurance of merchant ships assaulted by enemies in wartime. The gratitude of Lloyd's to Lord Nelson and his captains, expressed through its Committee of the day by the formation of Lloyd's Patriotic Fund, is ample proof of such quick response to pressing needs. A visit to the Nelson Room at Lloyd's will give one a vivid insight into the close relationship of two protectors, one military and the other commercial, to the benefit of the community. "Comforts" for Nelson's officers and men included silver plate of great elegance.

A more up to date case of rapid response by a Lloyd's Underwriter to a quickly changing scene comes via a United States Congressional Committee on Deep Ocean Mining, at which the author testified in April, 1977. The job was to explain to the committee that insurance could carry the risks on deep sea mining ships, relieving the American taxpayer from subsidising another commercial venture. This entailed ranging over the various sorts of insurance cover available to a deep ocean mining ship and its managers. The Chairman started question time with a request for elucidation of the cost of so many cents per cent that Lloyd's War Risk Underwriters had quoted to cover risks of confiscation and seizure by a foreign power, of the ship and its mineral cargo, of cobalt, manganese, copper and nickel. He wished to have this quantified, against a layman's background of comprehension.

In 1941, before being gathered into the ample bosom of the Royal Navy, a young Broker at Lloyd's lived in interesting times, insuring United States flag ships crossing the Atlantic through U-boat packs, and where the German battleship *Bismarck* was lurking. Details of the last transatlantic voyage, insured at a rate of $25 per cent were placed in front of the Underwriter, in order to guide him as to premiums charged in the recent past. As he picked up his pen to fix the rate for the next voyage the "Caller", who keeps Underwriters and Brokers in touch with each other over a loudspeaker, rang the "Lutine Bell" twice, for good news. Silence prevailed in the Underwriting Room to hear him say "Gentlemen. The *Bismarck* has been sunk." Pandemonium soon broke out and when it had died down, Mr. Toby Green, the distinguished leading Underwriter, was asked for "today's rate". He picked up his pen and wrote $10 instead of $25, a dramatic drop in three minutes.

Looking up from the blotter on the table before the Senators to the Chairman of the Deep Ocean Mining Committee, Senator John Breaux, to find him smiling proved that the question had been answered to his satisfaction. Later questioning established that insurance could not and should not impinge upon the responsibilities of governments.

This story is intended to lead the reader back to ocean pollution and the ability or otherwise of marine insurers to prevent owners and operators of pollution-prone ships from repeating their mistakes.

Ambrose Bierce defines "misdemeanour" in his *Devil's Dictionary*, as "an infraction of the law having less dignity than a felony and constituting no claim to admittance into the best criminal society". Insurance abides by laws, at an international level. It cannot make them, but merely guides law makers, with its knowledge and experience. Thus it is that a shipowner can trail a long history of claims and mismanagement from one insurance market to another, always avoiding a "penalty rise" in premium for misdemeanours.

At many conferences on marine affairs over the past ten years, speakers have again and again mooted the idea that insurance should "show its teeth" and impose penal terms on operators putting ships to sea unseaworthy as to manning and maintenance. With so many markets chasing a dwindling fleet of tankers, as the world comprehends its emptying oil reserves, penalty rates have become a luxury. Recently, a leading Lloyd's Underwriter pointed out that all the recent maritime disasters had been under the best ownership. One will have to look elsewhere in this book for the causes of this new development, but one hopes that the tired ghost of insurers being able to drive bad owners to the wall has been laid to rest, at least to this readership.

Many books have appeared about Lloyd's, its history, its present and its future, and before the 1960's blasted cobwebs away, otherwise good accounts were emasculated by the cautious removal of any interesting stories lest they gave offence. Many heads, including mine, teem with such stories. In the dark days of 1940, when American hearts grieved for London under bombing attack, all seemed lost, but the American Trust Fund, set up by Lloyd's in 1939 to give confidence, was a firm bastion of security. In this sombre climate, a leading American Fleet, Lykes Lines, was seeking annual renewal of its marine policies. Lloyd's and Company Underwriters were in the sub-basement during an air raid, underwriting by candlelight, and in this Dickensian atmosphere the leading Company Underwriter offered a reduction in rate to the owners, to demonstrate Britain's fighting spirit! This gesture had a profound effect, far wider than it merited in monetary size.

Another story, in the same year, concerned a diminutive Lloyd's broker, quite a little overweight, who became a Special Constable. He was on duty, with a police armband and steel helmet at the bus stop at the foot of Cornhill, not far from Lloyd's building when the conductor asked for his help. A passenger on the top deck of the bus refused to pay his fare, and would the Constable invoke the law? The small round man climbed the spiral stairs, looked at the large muscular labourer's uncompromising back, and came down to ask the conductor "how much was the fare?" I never saw him broking a risk to an Underwriter, but the necessary "give and take" between them must have been one sided.

The contact between Underwriter and Broker at Lloyd's is one of confidence. The word over the Lloyd's crest at the main entrance is "Fidentia". Good faith has shone out like a beacon from this place, and assaults on it hurt only the reputation of those who care little for the future, bringing small credit to themselves and the illusion of quick progress. This to me is alien to the aims and aspirations of this great institution, and will not hurt it in the long term.

*　　　*　　　*

The origins of the word "risk" are unknown but much debated. Its meaning to the insurance world is a fortuity that *may* happen, and not an event that *must* happen, that is foreseeable. Anyone who has read about the Second World War in the Far East will know of the terrible toll of transport aircraft flying over "The Hump", the Himalayan route between Northern Burma and China. This was a calculated decision made during a period of acute urgency, when supply routes had to be maintained at almost any cost in lives and materials. The Douglas C-47s Skytrains and Curtiss C-46s faced enormous upward and downward air currents over the mountains and valleys generated by extremes of temperature. They were often lethal, breaking off the wings.

In peacetime it would be unthinkable to take risks of such a magnitude, but the incidence of wilful neglect on the bridges of chartered tankers and conventional cargo ships belies this contention today. The well-documented demise of the *Torrey Canyon* thirteen years ago occurred when tankers were much smaller than they are today or five years ago. But it led to the strengthening of international law, to the temporary comfort of the marine insurance community among other parties. It has been obvious to all that there is no braking mechanism to international ignorance and wilful neglect by officers on the bridges of big ships, whose ships are managed by opportunists with no understanding of the savage nature of the sea.

An interesting comparison made recently on the publication of profit made by a major oil company, was that in one year it exceeded the premium income of the whole of Lloyd's, unrelated to profit or loss. The statistics on the loss of oil tankers and disastrous spillage are eloquent in demonstrating that there is serious imbalance between the two industries. It demonstrates also the importance of the insurance industry in correcting the trend. Oil spills by early 1979 had increased over the past five years by 300%, but the increase since then has been far greater, and is certain to be exceeded in the future with the knowledge available from present sources. No law yet made can encompass the increasing ignorance of good seamanship that is spreading, out of control, leading to wastage on a scale not even acceptable in war time.

The gap between the shipowning communities and marine insurers was a narrow one twenty years ago. This gap has widened increasingly in the recent past and communication between the two is virtually non-existent except with the few large fleets that are an unobserved example to those who are causing the chaos at sea. The yardsticks used by marine insurers to assess good and bad risks, having gone metric, are no longer germane. Attempting to solve them by computer is to court disaster, which many are finding out to their great cost. The problems are human ones, and cannot be analysed mathematically with any coherent result. Speeches made at shipping seminars are heard or read by very few insurers of ships, and the reverse is the case.

Hydrographic seminars, where the urgent need for survey ships with modern equipment is discussed, go unheard by both Parliament and the marine insurance community. Oceanographic seminars are reported but never reach either of these industries. Efforts at communication with western governments are baulked by day to day work, interfering with what seems to be the remote voice of problems in distant oceans. The problems of waste, spillage and the rising annual loss of lives are considerations that legislators representing all of us must consider urgently. If the chaotic state of traffic in the English Channel and its approaches, for example, were translated to aviation, no-one would dare to fly in commercial aircraft. An airline pilot 81 years old, or 73. A Labrador dog trained to bark when it saw another aeroplane on a collision course. An uncertificated aircrew with no physical or mental health checks. All these examples are authenticated and are less rare than is generally accepted among ship managers, aside from the public. However well-managed a fleet of ships, it cannot withstand the assaults of such stupidity and lack of ordinary safety strictures all over the world. Two of the most recent major oil spillages were caused by small ships hitting large tankers when they were at anchor.

A man who can employ a dog to help him navigate his 500,000-tonne ship can be counted on as being ignorant of the crude state of most nautical charts and many other hazards facing him. Many insurers of a wide variety of ships are just as ignorant; the "risks" they face are inevitabilities. The deliberations of a Court of Law presented with processed evidence cannot be termed "analysis" and this is particularly so when they are held long after the event took place, when it is obscured and rendered humdrum by many subsequent more newsworthy disasters.

To state that most accidents at sea in the past ten catastrophic years, since *Torrey Cannon*, could have been avoided is not wide of the mark. To add that no lessons have been learnt by those who need the advice most, is equally accurate. It would be tedious to list all such disasters, but a look at the most spectacular ones will illustrate the lack of interest in the Court findings, which disclosed ill-judgement at best and total avoidance of ordinary common sense at worst.

The Netherlands Maritime Institute has done and is doing a unique service to sanity in the oceans, by publishing findings on major disasters. Most public meetings after an oil spillage that has come to the attention of Members of Parliament or Senators, whose constituency has become oily, are an apologia, describing the spirited and successful efforts to salvage the ship or her cargo. Headlines sometimes reach the popular Press, such as *"Christos Bitas – The Success Story."* At the time of the accident, the Department of Trade withheld the evidence given sparingly by the Captain and by the time it was released public interest had been overrun by many new disasters.

The charterers of the ship, B.P. Tankers, stated through their Managing Director Mr. George King that the ship had made 200 voyages for his company and that only one of eight incidents in her career could be interpreted as the fault of the crew. On the other hand a *Times* correspondent reported that since the launching of the *Christos Bitas* in 1963 the ship had been involved in ten incidents before her terminal contact with the Welsh coast. He also reported that all attempts to discover why she had hit the Hats and Barrels rocks were met with refusal. The Department of Trade's official report made the point that it was not concerned with the reason for the casualty, which is a subject for an enquiry under the Merchant Shipping Act.

By the time that this delphic statement had been made the public

7) The *Christos Bitas* wallowing in the Irish sea after having hit the Hats and Barrels rocks. Some of her oil was successfully pumped out before the ship was sunk. (Keystone)

had forgotten the name of the ship that caused such havoc on the Welsh coast, and the graph depicting loss of precious oil into the sea, rose further in its deadly upward climb. Once again the real cause of this profligate waste of oil, money and wild life was misguidedly hidden by government officials in the murky fog surrounding "sub judice", which does not obtain in the air. The supposed cause of the Air New Zealand DC 10 crash into Mount Erebus in the Antarctic was made public within four days of the death of 257 people. The last three messages before the fatal impact were made available to the Press, and thus the danger of flying low in deceptive visual conditions was revealed to airlines and the public with vital immediacy.

3. Boredom at Sea

The problems of alienation have already been touched on. It is generated initially by boredom and the necessity of team spirit at sea, when the crew are in charge of a huge quantity of lethal hydrocarbons or explosive natural gas, for example. The case of the costly collision of the *Venoil* and the *Venpet* briefly described will serve as a starting point.

A conference was held in late 1978 in Southampton on Marine Simulation, the practice of manoeuvring miniaturised tankers as training exercises. The promotion of conferences has become an industry in itself and a growing coterie of professional conference-goers tends to swell these functions into big expense account money spinners for their promoters. Very little telling decision-making has emerged from the many I have attended over the past ten years. The Southampton conference was however deservedly popular, with 200 delegates and a hard core of experts in an important field. Bridge team organisation is the key to the reduction of a host of serious accidents at sea, as the *Venoil/Venpet* collision illustrated so eloquently. From this conference there emerged consensus opinion that most deck officer training was on an individual basis, and this seldom included training in team work. The same applies to passenger aircraft flight decks. The dreadful Trident tragedy at Heathrow in 1973, in which taped voices afterwards proclaimed flight deck confusion and acrimony, illustrates the breakdown of team training as being the prime cause.

A glowing example of an efficient and humane approach is, as mentioned earlier, provided by the Dutch salvage tug company L. Smit. This company has maintained a policy to recruit crew, town by town, or village by village, so that all the crew know each other and each other's families. Thus in a crisis, each crew member is intuitively in touch with his opposite number, and this has resulted in the acceptance of the Smit Company as being the most successful salvage tug company in the world, with happy ships as a natural side effect. There is no evidence to the contrary that this level of team work obtains on the bridges of the major tanker companies and cargo fleets. But for the rest one can go to the bottom of the scale of "togetherness", to a report of crew trouble in the good ship *Veesky*, arrested in Bremen in April, 1979, with the crew, after a voyage lasting some three months, claiming some $135,000 back payments. The crew consisted of sailors from seven nations. Such a Tower of Babel at sea is ludicrous, and it is not surprising that the engine room was reported to be under water. In 1969 the *Clara Clausen* was grounded on the North shore of the St. Lawrence River. After the Canadian pilot came on board and the course was set, a remark about the weather in English by the Danish Officer of the Watch was misunderstood by the Filipino helmsman as a helm order. As a result of compliance with the "order" the ship turned sharply, ran aground on the rocks and became a total loss!

Pride in being a seaman is a shrinking sentiment, except in the world's navies, where a uniform and a sailor's rolling gait still proclaim his pride and self respect. The boredom of a long voyage dulls the awareness and anticipation of seafarers on large oil tankers where mechanical routine is a weak generator of adrenalin. Lack of the deck duties and the community feeling that comes from physical effort with shipmates leads inevitably to malaise and a general feeling of a need for stimulus, and tangentially to a dulling of alertness to the explosive nature of the volatile cargo beneath one's feet. In the days of Captain Woodes Rogers, pigs were carried in pens on the decks of naval and commercial ships alike. It is well-known to farmers that these animals resort to tail biting when forced to exist in the fundamentally unnatural conditions of modern intensive breeding units. When given toys, such as chains, rubber tyres and piles of newspapers, they give up tail biting and thrive. A psychologist, Dr. Saul Gellerman, prepared a table of dull jobs for a business research organisation, with the preamble that dull jobs are nearly always the vital ones, but mistakes by bored employees can cost lives and millions in damage. One of the dullest jobs he listed was radar screen operators. Service in the British Navy means that one has an understanding of the mesmeric effect of staring at a green lit screen for any length of time. This leads to stress, which a conference on the subject pronounced to be common to a quarter of the workforces in industrial countries, leading to alcoholism, child abuse and even infertility. A Ford worker, some years ago, talking of making cars said, "It's the world's most boring job, it's the same thing over and over again. There is no change in it, it wears you out. It makes you awfully tired. It slows your thinking right down. There's no need to think. You just carry on. You just endure it for the money. That's what we're paid for – to endure the boredom of it". As the actor Kirk Douglas put it: "I don't have my children's problems – I was born poor".

The Pastor of the Norwegian seamen's church in New Orleans in an interview with the *Catholic Maritime News*, published in the United States, put it thus. "There is so much automation, so much more leisure time, isolation and loneliness. There is nowhere to go. They can't go home at 5 o'clock. It's the same problem that you find ashore. It seems that when people make more money and have a higher standard of living, they have more psychological problems".

It is ironic that Henry Ford said that "history is bunk" during a libel action in 1919, when in 1913 he had altered the course of it so radically with the timely (or untimely) re-invention of the conveyor belt and production line. I doubt if he was aware that two ships lay on the seabed off Sicily with clear evidence of a production line during the Punic Wars, over 200 years before Christ. Two warships were found by the famous underwater archaeologist, Honor Frost, providing clear evidence of paint marks on the outside of their hulls, proving that they were built upside down, and explaining why the speed of building a fleet took the enemy completely by surprise. The modern aspect of this fascinating discovery is that the soldier-oarsmen, through an excessive flow of adrenalin, caused no doubt by trying to do two jobs at once, resorted to cannabis to dull their fears and pain. Baskets of a type of cannabis were found in the wrecks. Equally, a low flow of adrenalin can lead to an intake of chemicals to produce illusion, euphoria and oblivion. In late 1970 the principal speaker at a maritime session of the International Labour Conference opined that one of the main problems arising from the then new automated ships may be heightened mental tension from the increasing amount of repetitive or controlling work and the need to work more in isolation from others. At another session of the same conference, another speaker said that what was being witnessed was not merely technical advance in regard to ships themselves, but a profound transformation of the entire shipping industry. What was then needed was an equally profound transformation in the shipping industry's attitude towards its human social problems.

That this challenge has not been met is eloquently proven by the lamentable increase of 40% in 1978 over 1977 in accidents at sea, the large majority of which were caused by human error, and a large majority of the errors caused by boredom, staleness, repetitive work and isolation. A notable exception was provided by the Captain of a 15,000-ton general cargo ship *Sea Moon*. His interests are photography, printing his own photographs, scale models, music, reading, model racing cars and ship prints. He records tapes for shipboard entertainment and much of his prize-winning efforts are devoted to improving shipboard social life. If most Captains at sea today had Captain Adsherd-Grant's imagination and insight, the soaring graph of loss of life, pollution and wasted money would soon start to bend downwards.

The excitement of a landfall to the deep ocean yachtsmen and women has been copiously documented and described in recent broadcasts mainly as to the dreams of hot baths, walks in pine forests and cool drinks. These expectations are an important element in mental stability and an incentive which is sadly lacking in bigger commercial vessels. It has often been said that there is no such thing as a *little* boredom. The poet Byron described the problem 150 years ago or so with society being "one polished horde, formed of two mighty tribes, the bores and bored". Factory layout is of great importance in reducing this menace, on land as the Swedish Saab motor company have proved conclusively, but bridge layout on big ships is even more so. Modern ships' bridges are a mass of navigational aids, internal and external telephones, smoke and fire detector panels and a host of other panels and dials. Many ships increasingly rely on automated systems, cutting down crew sizes. A 1976 West German Shipowners' Association study on the "ship of the future and its crew" suggested a 12-man crew on container ships and bulk carriers, currently manned by 30 crewmen. Three years later, a Japanese study advocated a 7-man crew for equally large ships. One hopes that the seven men have no personality clashes, with 702 feet to separate protagonists, if the need for privacy is pressing.

In 1972 a Mr. Joseph Begley of Evesham saved 2,000 cigarette coupons, posted them to a cigarette company asking for a watch in return, which never arrived. He wrote and asked why and received three watches, returning two. The next day, 10 parcels arrived, the following day 18 and the next day the local Post Office telephoned to say that 10 more parcels were waiting for him. All were gifts from the cigarette company, among them three tape recorders, a doll, a golf bag, two electric blankets, a carry cot, saucepans, a pressure cooker and long playing records. The victim of this munificence wrote a long pleading letter asking them to stop the flow. By return came a reply: "It was a computer error." The company gave Mr. Begley 10,000 coupons for his troubles. With these he ordered tools and a bedspread. He received a plant stand and two step ladders instead. "The computer did it again," a company official said.

Two years after Mr. Begley's exhausting tussle with a computer, a 30,000-ton tanker in ballast, the *Golden Swan*, was drifting six miles east of the South Goodwins without lights and with no navigational aids working, and engines stopped. This was in a busy part of the Channel at a busy time of year, with thirty thousand tons of ship not knowing where it was. Finally, engine repairs were made and the ship proceeded on her voyage, but the incident was not reported in any paper other than *Lloyd's List* with its specialist circulation. Reliance on machines in preference to men at sea received another severe setback. When battles between semi-automated ships and savage storm-laden seas are at their height, the loser is always the ship.

The metamorphosis from keeled ship-shaped vessels to all manner of odd shaped ones, making the loading of containers or barges easier, has been rapid, as a ferry trip across the English Channel will demonstrate. The sophisticated container ship *München*, of some 40,000 tons, was lost with all hands in December, 1978 north of the Azores, after the briefest S.O.S. No satisfactory explanation for this tragedy has come to light, but it seems probable that she was met by sea conditions that no ship ever built, with whatever modern technologies on board, would withstand. This loss will be referred to later, but I wish to make the point that the sea's savagery is much more majestic and awesome than most landed Ph.Ds can imagine when designing ships. No reflection on the owners of this ship, so tragically lost, can be made regarding her staunchness and her fine crew and management and their long safety record. The over-stretched hydrographers cannot be blamed for not surveying a little-used area of danger in storm conditions.

An interesting experiment in improving life at sea by the Master of the 253,000-ton supertanker *Esso Wilhelmshaven* is the building of a greenhouse high up on the superstructure. Captain Federico Scarati, using heat from the funnel and a lot of ingenuity, grows fresh green salads, tomatoes and flowers to brighten his crew's quarters. An oil rig in the cold wastes of Alaska is decorated with huge colour photographs of birch forests, dappled with sunlight, with potted plants, giving the illusion of a leafy glade instead of a cold piece of automation.

The efforts to prevent the spread of rabies to Britain have had a sad effect on the carriage in ships of animals as pets. The value of the relationship of man and animal can be well illustrated by the effect of the hospital cat on a girl patient suffering from paranoid schizophrenia, reported in the *Nursing Mirror*. The patient had become unapproachable and hostile, imagining that the staff were trying to poison her food. Hope of helping her was on the verge of being abandoned, when the girl was visited by Ethel, the hospital cat. The look of hostility and dislike dissolved into a smile, and whenever she became tortured with hallucinations, the cat was brought to her. The cat was a more effective sedative than anything in the drug cupboards, and after seven weeks the patient was discharged. The Nurse asked her out of curiosity what the cat had that the staff lacked. "She knew when to keep her mouth shut and leave me in peace." After the car had taken the patient home, the Assistant Matron said to the Nurse: "Fetch that cat to my office. I want to talk to it."

The relationship of animal and man stretches far into prehistoric times. Many prisoners owe their sanity to mice, spiders and any living creature. The therapeutic effect of animals at sea is more important as each ship equipped with computerised equipment is commissioned. Whether it is tropical fish, caged birds or cats, makes little difference, and the story of the schizophrenic girl illustrates how alienation can be bridged so effectively. A report in September, 1976 by the International Labour Organisation Maritime Conference commented on the steady drift of seaman back to land. One reason given was the "modernisation" of ship operations "resulting in depersonalisation which ends in mental opposition to the work, and finally indifference", with quick turnarounds in port adding stress and boredom. Around this time fear of the spread of rabies led to the banning of pets on many ships.

An increasing method of combating the insidious menace of boredom and its derivatives is the distribution to ships of film material, which can be dropped by helicopter onto the decks of moving ships. The multiplicity of languages to be dealt with is a handicap, but keeping in touch with the success of favourite football clubs is in itself a potent therapy promoting healthy subjects for discussions. The other side of the coin is, to quote from a television play's heroine, "T.V. is the greatest aid to sleep since darkness." The standard of film, if lowered, will be counter-productive in its effect on bored ship's crews. It could lead to a report similar to that made on a sub-standard engine room artificer which read, "This man should be treated as a case of condensed milk. Stow away from engines and boilers."

Most myths are invented and spread to maintain an unassailable advantage to an elite. So it is that the seafaring community invented and held on to the notion that women brought bad luck to ships and the men who sail in them. The Sirens charming unsuspecting mariners into casting themselves into the sea to their destruction is unlikely to be used today as an argument to keep women away from ships. That there are women in responsible positions at sea is now an established part of present day policy in the U.S. Navy, culminating in the first women in modern history to command a ship. Richard Hakluyt, in 1586, said "ships are to little purpose without skilful sea men". He would now be in serious trouble if he did not add to this all too modern dictum, . . . "and skilful sea women".

Isolation is an increasing menace to mental health as automation increases its grip on our lives. The loss of religious beliefs in the West tends to enhance the feeling of loneliness and depersonalisation. Within living memory ships were communities, with chaplains, doctors, a communal feeling, spontaneous theatrical entertainment and a family atmosphere taking its tone from the Captain. The connotation "a happy ship" was common. The emphasis was to keep both crews and passengers busy and thus alert and mentally and physically fit. When slide rules became extinct in the late 1950s and computers crept into the scene, the whole notion of community and "duty" went by the board, afloat as well as ashore.

In many cities and towns in western countries, the kind of urban village life that still flourishes in parts of London, New York and San Francisco for example, disappeared. High rise blocks of flats and offices with supermarkets instead of small shops led to a steep increase in social tension, which took psychiatry and psychologists by surprise by the extent of the problem. Slum clearance removed squalor but also the therapy of community life and the "confessional" of the village shops. This led to alienation and boredom, and thus vandalism and suicide. The pressures of noise or total silence tipped reasonably healthy people into mental illness and, to our great cost, these problems have not been confined to land.

The phenomenon of snow blindness is well known, but the effect of a white environment such as obtains in many oil tankers and merchant ships today has not been studied. Colours are well known as having therapeutic properties, some as stimulants and others having the reverse effect. A long voyage on a large structure with little impression of being at sea, and hardly any of motion, can be made nightmarish by a lack of colour in the living spaces and without pictures to relieve the clinical atmosphere. A junior engineer on a large tanker tells of his senior arriving in the mess at 5.30 in the afternoon, running round the ping-pong table three times and trotting to the bar where a gin and tonic was waiting for him. He asked the barman what day it was, and being told, said, "In that case I'll have a gin and tonic." This odd ritual was habitual and was not an inducement to confidence in the mental balance of one's superior officer, he opined. It is interesting to digress into aviation and the practice of periodic checks on the mental health of aircrew. Current information leads one to believe that only one airline insists on regular checks, in the United States for example. This came from an experienced pilot whom I sat next to on a TWA flight a few years ago.

Mental health at sea is vital to safety, as it is in the air, but in the long term far more is at stake at sea than on land or in the air on the subject of clear thinking in a crisis. The dictum states: "In the country of the blind the one-eyed man is king." On the bridge of a huge tanker, the mentally alert deck officer is the ally of safety, his shipmates, and the whole of mankind. As Burl Ives put it: "American cars will soon be run on the oil that they scrape off the beaches."

4. Ship-Shape and Ship Shapes

Britain's strong links with sea trade began with the earliest coastal bartering in flint and stone for skins and grain some 3000 years before Christ. The earliest "ships" were extensions of river-crossing rafts with wood and inflated animal skins providing buoyancy and the primitive sails providing motive power.

The shape of ships has been a subtle and ever-evolving process with discoveries being made in widely separated places according to local conditions and materials available. The introduction of the wood-working adze for example was as important an innovation to primitive ship builders and traders as the advent of steam power in the nineteenth century.

The Scandinavians made discoveries in the North Atlantic in isolation from the Venetians contending with Mediterranean conditions. There is archaeological evidence from the coast of California of Chinese junks making trans-ocean crossings. The hazards and fearsome dangers of these Pacific voyages in ships which were basically large rafts can be imagined. Meanwhile contemporary sea travel in the Mediterranean could be just as chancy.

In 1458 a Gabriele Capodilista wrote: "The fury of the wind drove the galley . . . so that the Captain himself was not without fear and gave orders to strike the main sail . . . thus they had to negotiate the huge waves as best they might . . . the pilgrims were so battered that they gave themselves up for dead, and not only the pilgrims in the galley but the sailors also."

The discovery of a wrecked Roman ship, which had a square hole cut into its bowsprit, proved the first use of a second sail enabling ships to sail closer to the wind. All these evolutionary discoveries were gradual and bought hard, and the loss of ships and men was fearsome, even when clinging to familiar coasts. Henry the Navigator's efforts to penetrate evern further into African waters led to casualties not just from disease and privation but from shipwrecks inching into the scale of suicide, until ship shapes were made less like upside-down houses.

The thread that links all these characteristics together is the commonly held respect for the sea as well as the Creator. A great leap forward came from the Viking longships which were built on rugged and seaworthy lines with keels capable of riding out Atlantic storms, and European shipping derived great benefit from such influence. Meanwhile, back in the rivers, derived from primitive raft origins, there appeared flat bottomed craft to carry liquids, stone, hay and all the necessities and luxuries to life from Central Europe to its sea ports and into its interior. These craft having a low freeboard and flat bottoms were not considered suitable for ventures into deep water.

Throughout history, ships have been adapted to the rigours of the sea and the rages of weather, and the care with which they were built made deliberate disposal like a 1944 landing craft unthinkable. Henry the Navigator had too large and expansive a mind to consider the conquest of rounding Cape Bojador, beyond which lay dark mystic powerful lodestones that would draw the metal bolts and fastenings from ships so that they would fall apart, to be a reality. Other more real hazards were rocky shores menacing coast huggers and fearsome offshore currents that led to the unknown.

Mankind learns little from his short history, which lengthens as to his upright stance, under the careful gleaning of Palaeontologists, but never in the understanding of the nature of our small planet. Many books have been written concerning missing ships in modern times. It is a popular subject but it also proves the ignorance of the devastating power of coastal currents meeting storm waves from remote places. The history of the shape of ships sharply reflects this lack of knowledge.

The numerous ships that litter the Mediterranean seabed loaded with amphorae bear repeated witness to the busy traffic in wine and olive over the centuries. The change from using bitter pitch to pine resin to line these earthenware thin necked vases led to the Greek taste for retsina, just as stinking Tudor fish made tolerable by vinegar led to present English fish-eating habits.

Carriage of goods in bulk was a long time coming, and the first tanker proper, the *Glückauf*, was built in 1886 to the order of a German oil merchant, Wilhelm Riedemann. She carried 2,600 tons of oil and a depth of 23 feet. She was ship-shaped, with her bridge amidships and carried sails to augment the power of her steam engines. She had nine main tanks, with smaller tanks above them to allow for the expansion of oils in hot weather, the sides of the ship forming the tank sides. They were separated from the boiler room by a coffer dam boxing in the cargo pumps for the oil. The *Glückauf* was in no way an adaptation of a river going vessel and it is a truism that adaptations at sea are the path to disaster. The steadying effect of masts and spars in the days of sail was of great importance acting like a pendulum, so that they make use of the effect of wind on water, rather than to fight across and through waves, as ships without sails are obliged to.

It was the oil tanker that drew away from conventional ship shape design when sailing ships were at last made to look ridiculous in the face of Sir Charles Parsons' steaming *Turbinia*, which sliced through the ranks of reciprocating steam-engined battleships at the 1897 British Naval Review at Spithead, at 34.5 knots. This outpaced the fastest reciprocating engined torpedo boats with ample power to spare, from three shafts with three propellers each. The steam turbine was the death knell of the commercial sailing ships which had clung on through the nineteenth century, both coastal and deep sea, but did not kill the notion of sail training ships in the twentieth century, still used by several nations to spread respect for wind and wave power.

Screw and paddle steamers clung to sails for some years but now there was also a limit to both tonnage and draught, and in 1882 Lloyd's Register of Shipping had specified that ships of 280 feet length and more should have watertight bulkheads to aid keeping afloat after a collision.

A technical debate opened as ships ever lengthened and increased in power, over bow shapes, and went through various theories put forward by pioneer naval architects, like Froude and his son in Torquay, England, studying frictional resistance of the ship surface underwater for the first time. Their use of models in tanks was a giant step forward in hull design, previously directed by tradition, ignorant of the resistance of water and wave on ship surfaces. These experiments were conducted between 1856 and 1865 when he persuaded the British Admiralty to build a testing tank. About this time Matthew Fontaine Maury, known as the "Pathfinder of the Seas", was studying ocean weather and it is estimated that his efforts in the production of weather charts of the Atlantic Ocean were saving $50,000,000 a year in ships and cargoes that would have been delayed, lost or damaged by stress of weather but for his guidance.

Warfare is a well known catalyst for the advance of science, and the wisdom of "lots of small" in terms of oil tankers soon became apparent when shipping routes were menaced by U-boats and powerful surface raiders. In the Second World War, the Japanese attack on Pearl Harbor boosted the 5 million deadweight tons of so-called "T2" types of tanker built in 1942 to 15 million tons in 1943, to keep pace with depredations by submarines. These ships with their precious cargoes of fossil fuel were singled out by experienced U-boat captains, and it would have been sheer suicidal folly to build bigger tankers, even more easily spotted from a periscope, over one hundred of which were scanning the North Atlantic for targets in 1943.

One of them, the *Schenectady*, built at the Henry Kaiser shipyard as their first "T2" tanker, broke in two at her berth after returning from her trials which demonstrates their vulnerability to torpedo damage. This is no denigration, however, for the "T2" tanker in its simplicity saved many lives and made a vital contribution to victory in the Second World War.

The leap from the 544 feet and 16,613 deadweight tonnage of a typical tanker in 1945 to the largest mobile object ever built, the *Globtik Tokyo* of 1973, 1,243 feet (379 metres) in length with a deadweight tonnage of 483,664 tons, was in many respects a leap made in darkness. This ship had a draught of 98 feet (28 metres) and

From Glückauf to Supertanker

Glückauf   310 feet
1886

Esso Copenhagen   470 feet
1939

Orissa   775 feet
1965

Globtik Tokyo   1243 feet
1973

8) **From *Glückauf* to *Globtik Tokyo*.**

a bridge aft meant that the Master was as remote from the bows as a football spectator over three football pitches from the game he is watching. Further, it is not ship-shaped, but flat bottomed, square-hulled and built in essence to the same principles as a river barge. This was in the heady days when engineering concepts were getting bigger and bigger, with the exception of dry docks and floating docks large enough to accept oil tankers of such vast proportions. Three years before the *Globtik Tokyo* was afloat, Professor Conn of the University of Glasgow said to a meeting of owners, shipbuilders and naval architects that "practice had outstripped theory with potentially risky consequences in the building of mammoth ships". His message did not carry into the minds of legislators and the age of the giant and ultra-giant tanker was upon a world oblivious to its lethal potential, spillages of oils and chemicals on a scale that was beyond our imagination or control.

In the year that *Globtik Tokyo* made her debut, a senior scientist from the Marine Biological Association's Laboratory at Plymouth propounded to the British Association that oil products were going directly into the ocean at 10 times the natural rate. Two years earlier, the Audubon Society in New York heard that enough oil and petroleum products were spilled into the oceans to provide 75 million cars with 20 gallons of petrol each. A year before that, in 1970, Dr. Max Blumer, senior scientist at the famous Woods Hole Oceanographic Institution in Massachusetts, stated that 10 million tons of oil flow into the sea every year mostly from oil-tainted ballast water dumped at sea, but also from rivers carrying tons of motor car sump oil. In 1974 the *Universe Leader* let 200,000 gallons of crude oil into Bantry Bay, the scene of the *Betelgeuse* explosion, pollution and the death of 50 men in early 1979. To prevent counter-productive over repetition, one could conclude with a remark from a petroleum industry spokesman in 1969: "In this day and age, there should be effective ways of controlling major oil spills and better yet, preventing them from ever happening . . ." He continued that "a growing group of Government Agencies, petroleum interests and equipment manufacturers are diligently searching for new ways of applying present technology to the control of oil pollution".

Never was diligence so ill rewarded. To claim that nothing has changed from the time that these high flown words were published is a pale reflection of reality. Every year statistics published by Lloyd's publications proclaim a record of ship casualties for that year. The arguments posed by scientists, tanker operators, marine Underwriters and forecasters of calamities to come do not change from year to year. Each is predictable and the identity of each proponent easily recognised by the trite nature of his or her pronouncement.

The fact that is never faced is that an enlarged river barge fully laden with oil in the hands of a ship driver is no match for the rigours of ocean traffic and weather. If one looks at the 15,000,000 tons of tankers built in 1943 and a vast number of cargo ships built at the same time, at great speed, then from whence came trained deck officers to man them? These huge ships of today are in essence enlarged barges with handling characteristics widely differing from conventional ships. One of these is the easily understood opposite of a speed boat lifting onto the surface at high speed. At low speeds, big tankers "squat", so that the 1870 chart marks, often ignoring spring tides and channel surges due to pressure during bad weather, lead to groundings. At low speeds these vast machines are barely manoeuvrable, particularly in a heavy cross wind, or current. A glance at the story of the Captain of the *Queen Mary* taking his ship into New York Harbour during a tug strike with the aid of a piece of wood embedded with nails to aid careful navigation by alignment with landmarks on shore will illustrate the issue better than many pages

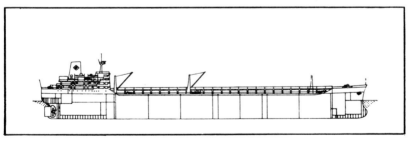

9) The *Orissa*, typical of mid-sixties tankers before the leap to gargantuan size. Engines and bridge are all aft leaving 500 feet of uninterrupted tankage before the ram bow.

of technical jargon. He had the advantage of a lofty well-sited bridge, but the tanker Captain cannot see under his own bows, nor correct swing in a gale, as the *Amoco Cadiz* told the world, to its cost.

To revert to the wand waving that produced so many war-built tankers in such a short space of time, their crews were perforce given only rudimentary training in seafaring skills. The ships were almost invariably in convoy, directed by experienced naval officers in protective escorting ships. Thus the notion became accepted, of merchant ships manned by men with the barest knowledge of emergency procedures, or decision making under stress. The war-built ships first allowed into European waters by the United States administration were not issued with charts of European waters, on the grounds that "all hazards were well known".

The spate of groundings is still a vivid memory to Members of Lloyd's in those far off days. The demise of the Lloyd's "Captains' Register" under a weight of legal actions and the complexity engendered by Captains switching from ship to ship, was a loss to sanity at sea. Tramp-ship owners and all of the largest tanker fleets had to be content with deck officers, with hard won wartime experience, but of scant use in peacetime conditions without a shepherd to shield them from the ocean's treachery if not the enemy's.

This notion is still with us, as a study of any Court report on a tanker accident will disclose, usually published many months after the accident occurred. These reports do not cover minor infringements such as that reported by the Captain of the Swedish 10,000-ton bulk carrier *Tunadel* off Canvey Island in July, 1978. As Captain Fred Martin approached the island he noticed a small fully laden oil tanker pulling out from the Shell Haven oil jetties into his path. Radio messages and blasts on the whistle were ignored and he was forced to swing his 460-foot long ship into the jetty to avoid a disastrous collision. The tanker passed close ahead and down the port side, and there was no person visible on the bridge, nor was any effort made to avoid a collision. At the time, the House of Commons was discussing pollution just up the road.

In 1971 it was reported by a thoughtful journalist that there was no international regulation to require the Captain and officers of a merchant ship to have any qualifications at all. Thus a deaf mute, blind to boot, could sail a supertanker anywhere he wanted, including the sandbank of his choice. A House of Commons Select Committee found recently that 75% of collisions and strandings were due to human error, and that no amount of technical equipment would alter the fact that the quality of seamanship was vital.

In these circumstances it is safe to imagine that only scant attention is paid to the weather. The number of shipping companies taking advantage of increasingly accurate weather routing techniques is relatively very small in terms of world-wide shipping routes. The ships that do take advantage of such careful routing to avoid storms save both fuel and heavy weather damage to their great advantage in reducing insurance claims and thus premiums. Weather routing is close to the interests and practices of the world's Hydrographers who regard looking for bad weather as supreme folly. The gap between forecasters and the shipping world is probably one of ignorance of the work done on their behalf at the weather centre at Bracknell in Berkshire. The centre is a focal point for information from weather stations all over the globe. Their work was not eased by the withdrawal of some key weather ships in the Atlantic, which give precious information on the progress of powerful storms and areas of low pressure. The case for advocating increasing weather routing of ships is growing in strength as satellites join the world's network of weather information. The growing trend of ships being manned by fewer and fewer men is just as important as a subject for weather routing, even if the ships are mere robots.

For large modern ships with crews of 30 to 40 men to disappear without either trace or signal of distress excites all kinds of theories, including "holes" in the ocean which can be discounted by a spell in one's own bath. There are various areas on the world's continental shelves, particularly at their edges, known as the "hundred fathom line", that are very dangerous when struck by storm waves. It must be appreciated in this context that the Admiralty and other charts are extremely crude in depicting accurate mapping of areas 100 fathoms deep on the continental shelves which surround each of the continents, in varying degrees of breadth and depth. The waves generated by severe storms, striking comparatively shallow water, throw up huge tongues of water, making equally vast troughs which are lethal to the biggest ship. The term "100 fathom line" is perforce only the vaguest generalisation, and one must bear in mind that glacial forces millions of years ago left battle scars on the sea bed as well as the surface, such as troughs, mounds of boulders and rocks and pinnacles. Thus it must be realised that despite the great heights of modern technology, the shallow depths of the world's continental shelves still require navigation to be an art and not a science.

The most dangerous areas to shipping are the busiest ones. Areas where giant waves occur, wrongly called "freak" waves, since they recur in specific areas, are not confined to remote areas, as records kept of missing vessels over five years demonstrate very clearly. There is a growing list of vessels suffering extreme damage off the South East Coast of Africa where the powerful southerly Agulhas Current meets storm waves travelling northwards from storm centres in the Southern Atlantic. The Hydrographer of the British Navy's warnings in the *Africa Pilot Volume III* go unheeded by the Masters of ships using this fuel-saving route. The amount of damage to ships in the area discounts any fuel saving by using the current by several orders of magnitude, as to lives lost, as well as ships and money. A list is tedious, but two examples will illustrate the lethal nature of the area during strong south westerly winds. These generate waves up to 8 metres (26 feet) in height, which if added to by a swell of greater length will create a steep-fronted wave that will swallow a 500,000-tonner without trace, always preceded by a deep trough into which the ship falls. The large tanker *Wilstar* lost her bulbous bow, swatted off by such a wave, off Durban in 1976. The British cruiser H.M.S. *Birmingham* was steaming comfortably in the area during the Second World War when suddenly without warning, she hit a "hole," and the next sea broke over A and B turrets and the open bridge, 60 feet above the waterline.

Many other ships have suffered far worse fates in this dangerous area where "episodic" waves occur and recur. A shipowner responding to an article on the general subject circulated it among his ships and the *Graigaur* experienced just such conditions off Newfoundland in November, 1976. The ship was prudently proceeding at 3 knots in a force nine gale, when suddenly she appeared to fall into a hole in the ocean, quickly followed by a huge wave that swept the ship from stem to stern.

Other areas where a consistent pattern of disasters occurs are to the south of where the *Graigaur* was savaged, on the Eastern seaboard of the United States. In this area four large oil tankers have been lost without trace, on a line from Cape Hatteras to the North East, and others have been broken in two with heavy loss of life, all in conditions similar to those experience by the British ship off Newfoundland.

In the winter of 1942 the *Queen Mary* was within an ace of disaster while on her lonely occasions off Greenland carrying some 15,000 troops. An eye-witness who was on the bridge at the time was one moment looking at the bows and the horizon and the next staring wide-eyed into a massive hole at a steep angle to it. This was followed by a huge mass of water which scraped everything off the bows and smashed through the thick toughened glass on the bridge like tissue paper.

The Captain of the *Leonardo da Vinci* tells of her sister ship the 44,000-ton *Michelangelo* suffering damage to her elegant bows and flooding the fore half of the ship in an episodic wave 800 miles from New York City. This would be well clear of the 100-fathom line and there would be no means of anticipating such a massive wave in mid-ocean. It would be the meeting of a long swell from storm waves reduced in their breaking power by distance meeting storm waves from another direction of different amplitude, resulting in "one on top of the other".

Two ships, the *Araba* carrying 1,300 tons of steel scrap, and the larger *Cretan Star* with some 28,000 tons of Arabian light crude oil on board, disappeared without trace off the north-west coast of India. Both were lost in September, two years apart, at the height of the monsoon. At this time of the year, the former Indian hydrographer, Commodore Kapoor, warns that the south-west monsoon throws heavy waves onto the continental shelf, making navigation across the area extremely hazardous.

Thus there are known areas, off Greenland, off the East Coast of Canada and the United States, off north-west India and off the south-east coast of Africa where a sufficient number of losses or reports makes the likelihood of waves of lethal magnitude a probability in swell conditions or stormy local weather meeting spent waves from a remote storm area.

For ships to avoid episodic waves is as difficult as avoiding earthquakes or any other majestic natural phenomenon. However, risks can be cut and a careful scrutiny of the Admiralty or other Pilot book of the area and the chart, are necessities to the avoidance of danger, keeping away from the outer edge of the continental shelf, or 100-fathom line in the conditions described.

Episodic waves revive speculation on old mysteries, such as the disappearance of the passenger liner *Waratah* in 1909, approaching Cape Town in bad weather, a classic position to meet an episodic wave. Since 1952, over fourteen large ships have sunk without trace in similar weather, and similar proximity to the 100-fathom line. Letters to the editor of *Lloyd's List* speak of similar conditions off Ushant, reported by experienced Masters, and the loss of the brand new fish factory ship *Gaul*, off north Norway, could well be explained by wave power of this kind.

Dr. Walter Monk and his colleague, Dr. C. S. Cox of Scripps Institute of Oceanography, are both authorities on the behaviour of ocean waves, both surface and undersea at great depths. They express the opinion that "the bottom contour, even at 100 fathoms, can influence surface waves, but only through its effect on the current. When the current is strong as with the Agulhas Current, off S.E. Africa, where more than 12 ships have been victims of episodic waves, or the Gulf Stream off the East Coast of N. America, any additional influences such as passing storms could compound the effects. There are other influences, such as refraction and the statistical probability that some waves in a train will be greater than others". Both scientists would require hard data on the environmental considerations at the scene in order to be more specific and mentioned the study being conducted by the South African Council for Scientific and Industrial Research. But exact positions are difficult to come by from ships sunk in 100 fathoms or from shaken survivors of badly damaged ships as to the precise geographical spot in which the wave occurred. Put beside the startling fact that well over half the British Isles has never been surveyed to modern standards, and that there are some 750 vessels of over 100,000 tons deadweight, one can understand the difficulties facing the South African oceanographers on the doorstep of a ship's graveyard.

The most practical answer given by both scientists and seafarers is slow speed, which minimises damage, as with the *Graigaur* off Newfoundland and the *Queen Mary* within a mere 5 degrees of disaster at speed, since the waves can travel at 30 knots. The most recent and tragic mysterious disappearance was of the barge carrying ship *München*, lost in the Atlantic in a storm some 450 miles north of the Azores with 28 souls after sending a brief S.O.S. A visit to the weather centre at Bracknell showed that the storm centre was close to the probable point of disappearance, and another visit to the library at Lloyd's to look at the chart gave a further insight into the probable cause. The storm centre and the ship were in the area of the Chaucer Bank. A call to the Hydrographers' helpful officers at Taunton gave the quick information that the 1850 discovery of water shoaling to 13 fathoms, resurveyed in 1959, had not been followed by anything more than cursory surveys, and no modern surveys have ever been made of the area. The Chaucer Bank is part of a volcanic chain of underwater "islands" that stretches into the Atlantic, but its position is doubtful. Evidently it is so doubtful that the American Hydrographer removed it from their charts, but Britain kept it and Germany followed suit. A further shoaling to 28 fathoms was reported in 1955 at the north western end, and 45 fathoms still further north. Any ship of any size in a force nine or ten storm, in which this ship found herself, over a bank shoaling to even forty fathoms, would be in deadly peril. Dr. Monk of Scripps' opinion of disturbance at 100 fathoms affecting the surface is germane to this theory. A further supporting fact was given by the owners to the leading Underwriter of the Fleet at Lloyd's, that one of the barges recovered had tell-tale marks on her keel plates. These showed that the barge had been scraped off from bow to stern, and thus the ship had not capsized, but gone in bow first. This leads one to think conclusively that she was met by an irresistible force of a magnitude that would overwhelm a ship twice her size. The route the *München* was taking was not a well worn track for commercial ships, but the presence of the Chaucer Bank and a severe storm is a perfect partnership for a savage episodic wave.

A recent article on episodic waves was dismissed by a leading authority on oil tankers, a member of one of the major British tanker fleets, as being of insignificance in relation to the number of ships at sea at any one time. This sort of rejection has unfortunately become a characteristic of those managing big fleets of big ships with excellent records, and the best training standards producing the best officers and cadets. The trend is to discuss disasters at sea as being statistically unimportant but it is acknowledged that well-run companies cannot comprehend the follies of less-well-run ones. The potential for chaos on the oceans is clear to a regular reader of the excellent periodicals *Safety at Sea*, *The Nautical Review* and *Lloyd's List* casualty section each day.

Turning from large natural hazards to smaller man-made ones, there are few statistics on the loss of containers into the ocean, or reports of large metal objects dropped from ships and barges laying pipelines on the sea floor, and ships that were thought to have sunk years ago but are still floating just beneath the surface. There were, in 1974, reports of a dozen or more abandoned derelict ships drifting in the ocean, a fruitful source for missing ships on the high seas. Early in that year a Greek ship the *Herakos* was rammed by one of these hulks whilst steaming southwards in the North Sea. Despite a ten-foot dent in the ship, photographed by Danish Coast Guard helicopters, and a three-day search by air, the ship was never found. In 1973 the passengers of an Italian liner during a Caribbean cruise were treated to the sight of the funnel of the 3,000-ton Colombian steamer *Duarte*, which disappeared in a storm off the Coast of

Venezuela 25 years before. She has been sighted nine times since the 1948 storm. The oldest such menace to shipping is the freighter *Dunmore*, which was abandoned in mid-Atlantic in a storm in 1908. She has been seen a dozen times, but always eludes the ice patrol and all other searches. Some of the hulks were abandoned by their Masters prematurely, by leaving the ship before it was necessary. Enough air is trapped below to keep the ship positively buoyant. The 6,000-ton *Montlucon*, a French ore carrier, was abandoned during a storm in the Indian Ocean. A few days later the ship was taken in tow by a Greek salvage tug the *Celcis* but broke loose in another storm and was presumed sunk. But in 1973, 22 years after, an Indian Air Force aircraft spotted the *Montlucon* drifting in the Bay of Bengal. This time she was taken in tow and made it to the breakers yard.

There are smaller floating objects than whole ships. In February 1977 a 35-foot steel pontoon was reported drifting in the ocean and in January a 335-foot derelict barge was sighted off North Carolina. On November 6, 1979, a British T.V. star, Hughie Green, had his cabin cruiser badly holed off Folkestone and despite hard pumping had to be rescued by lifeboat. The Captain who made the rescue said: "It was not a rock that caused the damage. There must have been something floating in the water. There is a lot of rubbish out there." On the same day a report in *Lloyd's List* stated that numerous units of pre-packed timber had been seen floating near a drilling platform off Aberdeen, and more bundles were seen to the north. There are weekly reports of large tanks, one 17 feet long, reported from passing ships and floating pipelines, as dangerous as torpedoes to small ships and especially so to wooden yachts. Boilers, concrete cylinders, pre-fab homes, and even a rocket cone have been reported floating in the sea. It is impossible to guess at the amount of timber lost in the sea, washed off deck-loaded ships in storms or heavy swells.

The dangers from wartime mines aside, in one year to January 25, 1979, no less than 270 containers were either reported lost overside from container ships or reported seen floating like icebergs, with only 10% of the mass showing above the surface. In December, 1976 the West German ship *Kini Keisten* lost eight 40-foot containers off the Lizard. In February the next year the steamer *Fortaleza* lost 29 loaded containers from her deck cargo during heavy weather, contents unknown.

The *Asia Freighter* had to anchor off Falmouth to take off 16 crewmen suffering the effect of an unknown gas escaping from a container. It transpired that two five-foot-long gas cylinders full of arsine were loaded into a container with tons of other machinery. The machinery was thought to have damaged the cylinders, causing them to leak the deadly arsenic-based gas into the crew's quarters. The gas cylinders should have been loaded on deck so that any leak would be dissipated into the air. In addition the cylinders were clearly marked with the skull and cross-bones, and labelled "dangerous", but being inside a container the warning was unobserved.

This accident sets the scene for further evidence of the chaotic method of packing and securing containers on and in ships on the high seas. The fact that the contents are unknown to the Master of the ship, and the method known as "groupage" mixes various consignments and incompatible materials and goods such as the ones just described, is a source of immense potential danger.

5. Owners and Managers

The changing style of ownership has had a dramatic effect on the shape of ships and the standards of excellence in the fields of navigation and ship handling, sending the graphs of those killed at sea, groundings, collisions, fires and explosions climbing upwards. Most people have read of Nelson and his captains, of the clipper ship era and *Captains Courageous*, and marvelled at the adroit handling of wind ships using the vagaries of a savage ocean to the best advantage. In the early 1900s, coastal craft in inshore waters of European countries and in United States and Canadian waters were a shining example of good seamanship in vessels that had been honed to efficiency through centuries of practical experience. The advent of steam, turbines, diesels and nuclear power in ships struck a mortal blow at traditional seamanship. Before, ships had had a beauty and grace that prompted poetry as well as the ancient call of the sea. Ownership was of the caring kind or at least understanding, and although tough, owners were frequently also drivers who understood the problems on the bridges and in the engine rooms of their ships. The size and draught from waterline to keel of these ships rendered them reasonably safe from gnawing rocks and wrecks, by using charts provided by hydrographers of the day that they used intelligently as advice to be interpreted, rather than followed blindly.

Ownerships of this kind are still extant, and many of the world's major oil company fleets follow these well tried paths of safety. But into this bland and lucrative scene stole owners of a different breed entirely who saw ships as mere shovels with which to dig profit from under the noses of the less nimble-minded. Ships altered their shapes radically, many becoming ugly, with sawn-off sterns and high bridges, haughtily surveying ill-secured deck cargoes as if nothing could hurt them, let alone toss them overboard. The tag from Richard Hakluyt in 1589, "Ships are to little purpose without skilful seamen", is more relevant to the present day than it was four hundred years ago. Now we have custom-built transport machines that are designed to be entirely functional in the sense of making quick profits, rather than to function safely in the ocean with its unpredictable and savage temper.

In 1969 at the prestigious Marine Technology Society's Annual Meeting in Milan, called "The Decade Ahead 1970–1980", President Nixon sent this message:

"It is the unknown frontier – the sea with inexhaustible riches – that will be the scene of the next great adventure of the American people. What little we know of the sea suggests here is a source of benefits so vast, opportunities so diverse, and power so immense that it rivals our previous frontiers of the land and the heavens. The Fifties were the start of the Outer Space Age, and the Seventies will be the start of the Inner Space Age, an age that will be unmatched in history, for challenge to man's ingenuity, benefits for the people of the world, and the sense of wonder that many have feared lost in the modern age."

One of the speakers at this conference said: "The paradox of the oceans is their role as both separator and unifier of mankind. . . . The oceans are no longer being seen as impediments to national development, but rather as vehicles to international development." From 1969 to the present day, each year has seen a steady increase in accidents, spillages of a wide range of oils and chemicals and wastage of assets on a scale that makes a mockery of the forecasts made in Miami ten years before. The spills increased 300% in the five years to March 1979. In 1974 there were 17 tons of oil spilt per tanker, by 1975 an increase to 45 tons, 50 tons in 1977, and 63 tons in 1978. These figures are from the Tanker Advisory Centre in New York, and can be assumed to be accurate coming from such a sound source.

The sea is thus becoming neither a separator nor a unifier of mankind, but a medium where the plunder of fish and minerals, attended by increasing pollution by spillages of all kinds, makes a mockery of its gifts to mankind.

One answer lies in Nelson's dictum, "Give me sea room". The continental shelves of the world must be avoided by ships in stormy weather. Even if the storm waves are often tired ones from remote areas of Antarctica, for example, meeting a strong current, such as the Agulhas off South East Africa, they can cause havoc on the surface. Information from Satellite Navigation Systems can be of great value in tracking storm waves, if the news is fresh enough for ships to take avoiding action. By and large, however, shipowners and Masters do not take the advice of hydrographers, much less oceanographers. The problem is exacerbated by ships built for maximum profit and not maximum seaworthiness, with owners whose only familiarity is with waves on graphs of profit and loss.

An important use of satellites has been shown dramatically in photographs of areas of the Indian Ocean made from several hundred miles out in space. These show, in the Chagos Archipelago, for example, that many reefs are shown on modern charts as eight and ten miles from where they actually are, and they reveal that reefs exist that are not shown on any charts, including one that is four miles long, shoaling to 40 feet. These reefs are another cause of "missing ships", but the speed with which such surveys can be made is a giant leap forward in the mapping of the ocean.

It is an absurd notion to ban ships of all sizes from the world's continental shelves. Long range forecasting however of the tracks of storms is within the range of present-day satellite techniques. The terrible toll of lives and yachts in the summer of 1979 during the Fastnet Race could have been avoided in the face of ample warnings from the London Weather Centre. The area south and west of the Scilly Isles, and the Labadie Bank, struck by storm waves is no place for any ship, let alone small yachts.

There is a constant hunger for books describing mysteries at sea, and the "Bermuda Triangle" is a favourite venue for many of them. There are quite enough mysteries to be solved, without inventing mysterious causes of disaster that simply do not exist. The "mystery" of the loss in July, 1909, of the *Waratah* off the South African coast can be explained by the number of other vessels lost over the continental shelf of South Africa when storm waves from the South Atlantic strike it. Other disasters can of course overwhelm ships with great suddenness, before signals can be made. The *Berge Istra* disappeared in December, 1975, but her loss in the Pacific was explained by explosions reported by two survivors. The owners were exonerated as to the maintenance of the ship throughout and the excellence of her crew was proved. A chain reaction of leaks, coming from pitted pipes, led to a massive explosion reaching the engine room and the ship was doomed.

The danger is that a "mystery" should surround the demise of a ship, when none exists and facts that could be gleaned are ignored. The owners of the *Berge Istra* would not be so puzzled as to the "bizarre" nature of their latest loss, including 40 well trained men, if they had consulted oceanographers at Scripps Institute, Woods Hole Oceanographic Centre, or a number of other centres expert in knowledge of wave behaviour. Some of the grieving dependants of the men lost in the new fish factory *Gaul* north of Norway believe that she was stolen by the Russians, but a careful reading of the reports of the time leads one to another conclusion. Her Captain was schooled by a senior one, who favoured running for port in foul weather. The Master of the *Gaul* was known to have turned in savage and worsening seas to make for port, and thus cross the shelf at the most dangerous time. That the ship was overwhelmed by an episodic wave seems highly probable and all the other ships in the area, going seawards, survived.

Almost every "mysterious" sinking of big modern vessels has a logical explanation when the right people are consulted, which they seldom are. Such circumstances are hard to be cured by legislation, since most legislators are just as ignorant, if not more so, of what obtains in the ocean, as the owners of seagoing ships.

Legislation is a two-edged weapon. If it is produced by legislators with only rudimentary knowledge of the subject, it can be over complicated in its efforts to disguise ignorance by using high flown language. The responsible tanker industry, worried by the accident record of less responsible owners, is fearful of legislation which will inhibit fair trading and fair profit in a difficult financial climate.

There are complications, however. One of the tried weapons used in the defence of pollution-prone fleets is the discovery of such phenomena as the recently discovered oil-rich layer hundreds of miles long and hundreds of feet deep in the South Western North Atlantic. This vast patch is estimated to contain over a million tons of crude oil, apparently from a natural oil seep from the ocean floor. It is thought to spring from the Venezuelan or Trinidad continental shelves.

Such discoveries are a gift to bad management and a blunt instrument to bludgeon arguments against careless or plain idiotic practices at sea. A sea officer of a cross-Channel ferry for example stated recently that in one week's tour of duty he had experienced four occasions when blatant neglect of international collision regulations had forced him into an alteration of course and speed to avoid disaster. Ferries normally have precedence in all circumstances. The vessels were a Greek and a Liberian tanker, an East German cargo liner and a large Dutch tanker. He went on to say that there was nothing new in such reports, and is the common experience of navigators in crowded waters all over the world. It illustrates a serious professional competence and watch-keeping vigilance. Criticism of British officers is not nearly so common as of some other nationalities, but it takes two to make a collision and the sea is no respecter of nationalities. An interesting exercise would be to find out if the owners of these vessels were made aware of such breaches of international rules and such breathtaking near misses that occur on a daily basis in many congested and also uncongested areas.

In 1972 a report from Washington was published in London, stating that one 60,000-ton ship sinks every day, that the world's sea lanes are becoming congested and the congestion is worsening due to the then increasing size and length of ships, that there is a growing disregard for safety at sea, and a neglect of the rules of the road brought on by economic pressures to move ships in and out of ports as quickly as possible.

1972 was a year when comparatively few vessels were lost. In 1978 world marine losses exceeded one million tons for the first time in history. 1979 was an even worse year, the figure tragically added to with the loss of the *München* on December 13. The decade ahead, 1980 to 1990 statistically will bring a rising graph of pollution and loss of lives and ships.

A consideration that must not be ignored on the subject of tanker losses on the world's continental shelves is the long term pollution aspect of ships lost in comparatively shallow waters. A ship when mortally struck on the surface does not sink like a stone, but "planes", forward or backwards, according to the whereabouts of the damage suffered on the surface. Thus a ship lying on the seabed may be some distance from where it sank below the surface, and it may be upside down, on its side or on an even keel. At depths below the average 100-fathom line the ambient temperature is so cold that oils of most viscosities common to crude oils become like hard cheese, and remain in the ships' tanks or bunkers molesting neither fish nor coastal areas, nor bird life. But ships sunk in shallow waters are a long-term menace to future generations of fish, birds and mankind, since the presence of oxygen excites the spread of rust and the presence of strong alkalis in the oil causes corrosion on the inner side of the ship's plates. Thus the oil may take years to escape, and the argument of natural ocean seepage, continuous since ancient times, is raised to cover these delayed action slow fuse seepages that are a problem for our grandchildren to face.

The changing style of ownership that has occurred in the past twenty years includes the vital business of training deck and engineer officers of sufficient quality, resourcefulness and efficiency to deal with emergencies such as collision avoidance and the correct interpretation of scanty chart information. The Captain of the *Argo Merchant* was well off course when the ship struck the shoal waters off Nantucket and broke in two, spilling millions of gallons of oil into the Atlantic fishing grounds, and was bluntly criticised by a U.S. Coast Guard Commandant, Owen Siler. His opinion was that Captain George Papadopoulos, whose ship had a record of 18 groundings in fourteen years, "had all sorts of equipment on board that he didn't use". This mid-December Christmas gift to the fishing grounds, 7.5 million gallons of heavy fuel oil, was not a result of good bridge training nor evidence that there was knowledge on board of the crude nature of nautical charts aside from knowledge of one's whereabouts in the ocean.

The Captain, a 43-year-old Romanian Greek, had sailed the previous nine years in Onassis tankers. He was two days behind schedule, and his tanker was costing £2,700 a day whilst at sea. The charter was worth £82,000 cash on delivery, so he pressed on at full speed, with water becoming progressively shallower from the echo sounder readings, hoping that it would still be dark enough to take an accurate star fix at 6.15 a.m., on a December night. At 6 a.m. and at 12 knots, 28,691 tons of ship struck a shoal off Nantucket. She was eighteen miles off course and had been well and truly "lost" for the previous 15 hours. Imagine an airliner approaching its destination with the pilot not knowing where he was, with most of his navigational aids not being used and 120 passengers in his care. The mind boggles.

An interesting equation is to look at the "economic" speed of a 500,000-ton tanker, produced from a study by a shipping company in 1970, and the present day training programmes described in October, 1979 at the Nautical Institute. Captain Donald Hindle told his audience that his generation were required to spend 3½ years at sea and six months in college during cadetship. Some Asian officers had experienced the exact opposite. They spent 3½ years in college and six months at sea. Putting a young officer in charge of a ship of 500,000 tons with six months at sea is lunacy of an extraordinary kind.

Training programmes for ships' officers are the duty and responsibility of shipowners, and there are shining examples of such good seamanship in high places among the major oil companies such as Shell, B.P., Gulf Oil and Exxon. But when smaller owners, growing like mushrooms, enter the shipping arena, there is no such careful attention to the finer details of the problems facing ships at sea. There are ship manoeuvring arenas in Swiss lakes, where Captains can simulate collision avoidance, but these do not add any knowledge of the correct interpretation of crude nautical charts, nor the "squat" of big ships at low speeds. Training has become a luxury on the oceans of the world and the rising graph of accidents will continue to rise year after year, hand in hand with chemical and oil pollution of the seas and rivers.

The pressures on the Masters of tankers managed by small companies chartering their ships to bigger ones are a main cause of casualties at sea. The *Argo Merchant* followed the path trodden by the famous *Torrey Canyon* in hurrying towards disaster, blind and unaware of any danger confronting them. The rarity, in the case of the *Argo Merchant*, was that the Master and several of the ship's officers were brought to book by a knowledgeable Maritime Court who penalised them, making an example for others. But it is not rare for the owners of a vessel causing a severe pollution to hide from public scrutiny in court, behind numerous charterers, so that the real ownership is never traced. As a New York maritime lawyer said at the time, "Everyone is trying not to own this ship."

The old saw "ships are all right, it's the men in 'em" no longer holds water among many owners around the globe. To them, a ship is merely a dot on a graph or mark on a computer readout that must spell "profit". That they can purchase insurance for very little outlay in many marketplaces throughout the world compounds their proneness to "accidents".

In July, 1979 a conversation took place, reported by a London magazine, which went thus: "I need an oil tanker, can you help." The leading shipbroker assured, "Yes, but what rates are you willing to pay?" "Anything", came the reply. "The sky's the limit. Just charter me one if you can." This method of conducting affairs at sea gives carte blanche to bad management when a ship is regarded as a large tank of oil to be moved from one port to another regardless of wind, sea, rock, fog or any other practical consideration. A report in the *Financial Times* described ship loans rivalling property loans in desirability, the amount of debt standing at around $38 billion, $5 billion of which is unsecured debt, and could be twice such a figure. This is one reason, it was reported, why shipowning is full of either flashy or highly secretive tycoons. These are men who thrive in the highly competitive private enterprise of modern shipping, when half a generation ago many shipowners had seen long service at sea themselves. With men at the helm of companies running 500,000-ton ships, seeing them as methods of making a lot of money quickly, the morale of the crews is a minor irritant. This morale takes further knocks from many sources, but the most potent is the current irreversible trend to man ships with computerised systems to reduce the number of men needed to push them across oceans.

The speed with which ships are built under these conditions of hurry produces some startling results. A number of Japanese-built ships were pronounced unsafe according to a Japanese seamen's Union in the late 1960's. The reason given was that the steel used in construction of the ships was of insufficient strength. This followed the disappearance of two giant ore carriers, *Bolivar Maru*, 54,000 tons in January, 1969, and the 34,000-ton *California Maru*. When the Japanese built the first supertankers no-one knew at the time the effects of the sea on the vast holds and tanks of big tankers and oil tankers. An 810-foot long tanker, the *Tamano* was anchored in the centre of a rapidly spreading oil slick in Portland harbour, Maine, one of the busiest oil ports on the East Coast of the U.S.A. It was later found that the ship had grazed the Soldier ledge with the bridge officers all blissfully unaware, and this gentle graze had punctured her thin plates, allowing 40,000 gallons of No. 6 fuel oil to escape. The major oil tanker fleets of the world use well-known highways and have highly qualified officers on their bridges, but the lesser ones are forced by freight indexes to be more venturesome. They thus venture into areas that make "squat" at low speed a very serious hazard and navigation in ill-charted areas positively lethal to even the biggest ships.

An event that puts the problem facing indifferent legislators into the clearest perspective was the *Independentia* disaster that occurred between the Black Sea and the Marmara Sea in November, 1979. It had been assumed that yet another oil tanker Captain had made a serious error of judgement, which is considered not to be news-worthy. It was reported by an eye witness that the splendidly managed Romanian tanker was *at anchor* about 100 metres from a breakwater when she was hit, waiting for a pilot to help her through the 875-yard wide Bosphorus. The Greek freighter *Evrialy*, of a mere 5,000 tons

10) The *Independentia* blows up off Istanbul. (Safety at Sea)

gross, had just completed the Bosphorus passage and her captain later stated that he had signalled several times to the tanker requesting her to give way. A ship requesting another at anchor to give way is, to say the least, a curious request. In the early morning there is little or no local traffic in the area, and conditions were good. The ship struck the tanker and a small explosion was followed by one that rocked Istanbul, and left the tanker a ball of fire. She had not been fitted with an inert gas system which would have reduced the magnitude of the explosion and perhaps the dreadful toll of lives.

This "accident" sets at naught the contention that the crewing of the majority of tankers offered for charter is responsible for most of the accidents that result in serious pollution or danger to large cities. The event that could have devastated Istanbul can be compared to a 5,000-ton missile being launched carelessly at a vast mass of volatile storage tanks.

The potency of tanker disasters to stir and affront the imagination has been dulled by their very frequency, obscured by trivia in the world's news media.

It has been too easy for too long for unscrupulous owners to buy insurance in a far too competitive market and to put ships to sea that are lethal menaces to well-run ones. For the major fleets to cooperate in their refusal to charter any ship whose Master and bridge officers fell below their own high standards, would transform the chaos and carnage of today into a sane tomorrow, in a matter of months, yet there would still be a legacy from the 1960's era of "whizz kid" shipowners, which led to ill-found ships and ill-found crews.

The speed with which containerisation hit an unready world makes improvement in this form of pollution more difficult. It is difficult to remember docksides stacked with all shapes and sizes of crates, cartons, boxes, packing cases and tractors, before the "container revolution" arrived. Up to the mid-sixties, ships were tailored to meet the worst kind of weather, and deck cargoes were insured at double the rates applying to cargoes in the holds. Increasingly, ships

11) A close-up of the *Independentia* blazing in Istanbul harbour, close alongside a jetty. (Safety at Sea)

were designed and built by naval architects whose grasp of the forces at sea was largely theoretical. Ships were adapted to the amount of containered cargo they could carry, rather than the amount of pounding they could take from force nine winds and waves. People with an intimate knowledge of seafaring drew further and further away from the shipowning community, and losses of deck cargoes increased as a consequence.

The vast and widening gap between science and commerce at sea is one that must be bridged if mankind is to survive into future generations. Pollution is only one lash of the flail that is castigating the oceans. Overfishing to a degree that makes cod a rarity to the people of Labrador and Newfoundland is a tragedy. Hoovering shoals of fish during their adolescence or reproductive season has become a general practice in many countries and can only lead to disaster. The warnings of those who study the life cycles of the fish we eat and those they live on still go unheard; at least the science of husbandry must be driven home to those who gather fish, if not the farming of them, practised by the Japanese for 2,000 years. But again, with fishing, the commercial and national concerns compete against each other with scant knowledge of the effect of their indiscriminate plunder of the dwindling resources of the ocean.

Of course there are voices of reason. Calls for curbing pollution, to curb overfishing, to encourage traffic lanes in busy bottlenecks, such as the English Channel or the Malacca Straits, have been frequent in the world's press over the past ten years. Single facts make their own impact – one in three of all ships passing the Straits of Dover carries something highly dangerous. This includes 1½ million tons of oil per day and 15,000 tons of chemicals. In 1963, I.C.I. started a service carrying liquefied ethylene gas from Teesside to Rotterdam in a 600-ton ship. The Dutch authorities were so alarmed that they labelled the ship "a floating bomb" and insisted that it be painted bright red and carry yellow fever flags to warn all other shipping away. Now liquefied natural gas tankers, potentially a far more dangerous hazard, have become commonplace, with no warnings to other ships of their explosive cargoes.

When a crisis develops there are techniques and equipment available which can control it. Speed however is of the essence. A real grasp of the "fire brigade" nature of the crisis was shown by an American company based in California, who were ready and willing to go to the aid of the South African Government in 1971, when the 50,000-ton tanker *Wafra* grounded on the Agulhas Reef with 40,000 tons of crude oil on board. Efforts were made through the South African Embassy in London and with the South African Government, but these resulted in the crippled ship being towed out to sea. She was then attacked by missile-firing Buccaneer strike aircraft much like the British Government's inept bombing of the *Torrey Canyon* in the spring of 1967. The rockets set the ship on fire and she was then finished by depth charges dropped from a Shackleton, which sank her to pollute another generation's environment. The air-droppable salvage pumping and storage system was and is refreshingly simple. It could be flown to any part of the globe in a cargo aircraft and then helicoptered to the deck of the stricken ship, dropping pumps and large 500-ton capacity rubber containers of extreme toughness to carry the oil pumped out by mobile pumps and towed to safety. The idea was taken up by the U.S. Coast Guard and re-christened "Adapts": air delivered anti-pollution transfer system. It had a chance to prove its very real worth in one of the most remote and lonely spots on earth in 1974, when the 206,000-ton tanker *Metula* hit the Satellite Patch at full speed of 14.5 knots. A United States Coast Guard strike force of six men was flown from New Orleans in a C 130 aircraft and used one of the pumping systems to off load some of the oil into small tankers which later delivered 50,000 tons of the oil safely to Quintero Bay in Chile. This quickly assembled kit could have saved much of the anguish generated by the *Torrey Canyon* and the *Wafra*, and it was a total lack of understanding by senior legislators that led to the disastrous pollution caused by both these ships and later the *Amoco Cadiz* on the coast of Brittany. During correspondence with the inventors of the "Adapts" system it became quickly evident that it could be carried by tankers at very low relative costs to pump oil overside into rubber containers instead of the defenceless ocean, before rocky teeth could gnaw their way through their ship's plates to spill her oil. At the time, the inventors were mooting the notion that insurance rates could be reduced on tankers carrying such effective anti-pollution equipment, but in 1973 the world was not preoccupied with the effects of oil spillage to the extent that it is today. The carrying of quick, simple and quick-acting pumps and flexible easily stowed containers that have reinforced bows to withstand heavy towing surges caused by wave action would be a huge advance in the prevention of spillages if it were taken up by the major oil companies and its simple efficiency understood by legislators and Underwriters alike.

A problem in the nature of a slow time bomb is the sinking of tankers full of oil on the continental shelves, where oxygen can join the strong alkali rusting the outside of ships' plates with the oil attacking the inside to spill oil far into the future. Some time ago the

Ecuadorian Ambassador in London enquired over the fate of the oil that could wreck his country's fishing industry. The ship was the *Jersey States* which suffered an explosion on the line dividing the waters of Ecuador and Colombia. The ship had taken some time to sink, with its engines intact after abandonment, and the whereabouts of the wreck with its oil was vague. It was suggested that a manned submersible operated from a mothership could locate the wreck with comparative ease, but the cost of mobilisation proved too big a hurdle. Technical help was given when an experienced underwater consultant was brought into the discussion, pointing out that the cold water at the depth in which the ship was known to lie would keep the oil at the consistency of cheese and, with no oxygen, corrosion would not be a hazard.

At lesser depths than that in which the *Jersey States* was lost the problems are greater, and the successful transfer of oil from the sunken tanker *Boehlen* in 360 feet of water 35 miles off Brest in Brittany was a heartening step forward. The main difficulty in recovering the 9,000 tons of Venezuelan heavy crude oil, called "Boscan", was its tar-like consistency. It had to be "melted" with hot water in order to be pumped to the surface, but this was done successfully by a well known French diving company in 1977. Below this depth of 360 feet (110 metres) there would be great difficulties in the recovery of a wide variety of oils as to their stickiness or otherwise. The loss of a number of ships on the continental shelves, which average 600 feet in depth, is a hazard that our heirs will have to face and overcome.

Maritime commerce is being sucked into a vicious circle of accidents of ever-increasing severity. There is no method of avoiding what will become a devastating vortex other than action from within the tanker industry. Legislation is too remote to control the habitual undertaking of ill-considered risks covered by myopic or uncomprehending insurers. The rising graph of collisions, groundings and explosions at sea does not merely embrace oil spillage of varying grades and viscosity, but includes chemicals some of which are malignant in their effect on sea life. These include nuclear waste and other radioactive substances carried into the chaos of roulette in the

world's shipping lanes. An example of the feeble spearhead of in-
effective legislation is the boarding of tankers in British waters, for
sporadic inspections by Governmental Marine Surveyors. They
board tankers managed by large safe fleets and pronounce the
vessels "seaworthy" in all respects, not comprehending that such
shipshape and Bristol fashion vessels are light years away from
vessels open for charter, where standards are lowered as expenditure
on modern officer training and navigational aids dwindles in the
shrivelling winds of low freight rates. The failure to distinguish
between vessels managed from small offices in the cheapest possible
way, with the ships cutting corners to meet tides, and those from
large stables with strings of thoroughbred ships and crews, spreads a
blanket of false respectability over the whole shipping industry,
which is a grave disservice to good management. The elasticity of
statistics produces an impenetrable web around the real issues.

The first rivulets in the flood that must float the Ark of sanity at sea
are visible through the cold blizzards of inept legislation that bewil-
der rather than clarify. The British Advisory Committee on Oil
Pollution at Sea recently advocated stricter control over British
companies and nationals who charter sub-standard ships. Thus,
while being a cry in the wilderness, it is among the first manifestations of an insight into the realities of the fundamental causes of
pollution of the oceans.

A much more heartening movement has been generated by the Oil
Companies International Marine Forum (OCIMF) whose Chairman of its Steering Group, to guide the various parties, is with Exxon
whose fleet of tankers has an enviable reputation. One of the main
brakes to safety at sea has been the consistent reiteration by major oil
companies who run tanker fleets that all is well at sea, and their
training programmes are second to none. These bland assertions
usually have followed a major accident to a chartered ship. The
assertions are enlarged by denials of any connection between them
and the author of the disaster. The initiative of the Oil Companies
Forum, spearheaded by an experienced tanker manager, has already
produced a result that deserves the widest acknowledgement.

Another encouraging sign came when it was reported recently

12) *Amoco Cadiz*, the aftermath. (Popper)

that the oil companies are concerned about the hard political and economic consequences of being associated with sub-standard tankers and pollution. A classic example was again the very large crude carrier *Amoco Cadiz* that ran aground with devastating effect on the coast of Brittany. The Shell Company, owners of the oil cargo, suffered significantly in the French market, despite the ship being a modern and sophisticated tanker. Thus charterers became even more aware of the need to hire tankers with a good well-trained crew, with the ship in good shape, shunning help from Labrador dogs on the bridge. In furtherance of this initiative a London firm of shipbrokers, John I. Jacobs, has mooted a "Tanker Register" yielding up-to-date information of the state of ships and crews to distinguish the wheat from the chaff. Thus the careless owner would quickly be starved of charters and the rising graph of accidents, loss of life and pollution at sea would at last begin to subside.

If the practices at sea that grew from the flood of war-built merchant ships and tankers into the commercial field, with ill-trained Masters, deck officers and navigators, were applied to commercial aviation, few people would be willing to fly. Aviation accidents are usually investigated soon after the event, with a quick advantage of "black boxes", but those at sea, through long delay, do not catch the public imagination. Even so, Aviation Underwriters are seldom willing to fly in chartered aircraft, preferring regular airlines. It would daunt the most hardened passenger to find the aircrew of three different nationalities communicating with each other with difficulty. But such conditions are common in many ships at sea today that exist on charter work, and the dilapidated state of essential equipment is only reported in technical publications with a small circulation. Such reports seldom escape from their restricted circles, and the despair of the world's hydrographers at the careless abuse of their nautical charts is only reported in small-circulation journals.

In terms of a cohesive effort to prevent the lethal trend of maritime disasters, the escape routes of the common sense and good seamanship advocated by knowledgeable people writing in technical journals were and are blocked by incomprehensible legislation. Politicians are usually insulated from the realities of present-day life and death at sea, and rely on information presented to them by advisers. First hand knowledge of inept and unworkable maritime legislation particularly in coastal waters is readily available to those that seek it. In order to gather up the necessary information for potent statutory instruments, the research departments of Ministers and Senators deluge the shipping industry with questionnaires and instructions on new legislation that inevitably confuse and yield the opposite result from that intended. The two sides are seldom in communication in the real sense, since on the one side are theoreticians searching for material that is usually fed to them by observers of minimal perceptiveness, and on the other side, practical seamen. There are of course exceptions to this lack of communication, but they are sadly few, and their zeal and understanding are seldom recognised by transient politicians running Ministries or Departments, for example.

Regulations that were brought into force in the Straits of Malacca, used as a shorter route from the Persian Gulf to the Far East, the alternative being the Sunda Strait between Java and Sumatra. Collisions and groundings grew in frequency and seriousness and leading to a traffic separation scheme endorsed by Indonesia, Malaysia and Singapore. These instructions to tankers large and small were so complicated that the common talk among hydrographers was that collisions and groundings were increasing because of the complexity of the rules rather than diminishing. If one reflects that the Japanese-built *Universe* class tankers draw 80 feet or more and need 90 feet in protected water and 100 feet in the open ocean, the scale of the Malacca Straits problem can be gauged. These ships are in shoal water the moment they come over the continental shelf, and they are not by any means the largest. Push these into the Malacca Straits, traditionally the home of coastal fishing boats, and the complexity of manoeuvring over these shoal waters becomes immediately apparent.

6. Menace from Containers

In a speech to a small but distinguished audience in California in 1970, I coined the world "imploit". An example of imploitation was the remarkably successful experiment of the Frankfurt Zoo, which bred gorillas in captivity and later released them into the rain forests and mountains of the Congo, where these magnificent creatures had been decimated by hunters. Imploitation is an attitude of mind, which in my view should be cultivated in the 1980's and beyond. It is the reverse process of exploitation, which seeks to extract the extractable and leave the husk of a once beautiful site to scar the earth. Examples of the exploitation of the land are easily discernible, but at sea it is more difficult. The deepest part of the ocean in the Americas is the Puerto Rican Trench, and photographs from these extreme depths reveal even here all manner of banal human detritus lying on the bottom from lavatory pans to flashlight batteries.

Travelling in transatlantic liners is sadly a thing of the past, and the charm of this way of crossing the ocean has gone for ever. However, a facet of such a way of life was the nightly dumping of mountains of garbage over the stern. It is an interesting reflection that passenger ships using the Suez Canal introduced sharks into the Mediterranean, following the bonuses of food thrown over the sterns of ships at night. Much of this rubbish does not sink, and any beach almost anywhere testifies to the careless use of the ocean as a dumping area, with plastic bags, boxes and bottles that are virtually indestructible littering the shores.

By scanning the casualty pages of Lloyd's List over a period, a pattern of careless release of all kinds of flotsam is revealed. The most prolific source of such menaces to small ships are the oil pumping platforms, around which divers' lives are hazarded by all manner of jetsam, from metal pipes through generators to tangles of wire rope. At a cost of £15,000,000, five hundred tons of scrap was cleared from the sea bed around drilling sites in Norwegian waters in late 1978. Plastic rope and cord can be a menace to miniature submarines, both manned and remotely controlled, as well as surface ships' propellers.

There are frequently reported sightings on the high seas of large metal tanks, of ungainly Dan buoys, of long metal pipes plugged at each end, and, of course, containers. The sight of many modern container ships, with three- and four-tiered deck cargoes from stem to stern would bring troubled looks from seamen of only twenty years ago. The 270 reported as either lost or observed in 1978 must be the tip of the iceberg. The flippant snooks cocked at North Atlantic storm-driven waves of huge power by many operators of container ships proclaims their total pre-occupation with loading and unloading and ignorance with what occurs in between, in the open sea.

In April 1978 there was a Press report that a mysterious gas cloud had killed sealions, fish, horses, cows and dogs along a 286-mile stretch of the Brazilian and Uruguayan coasts. Authorities from both countries sent specialists to determine if the ammonia-like gas originated from a natural chemical reaction in the South Atlantic, or from pesticides and bottled gas that sank near by. The deadly cloud struck people with fits of nausea and dizziness, one man dying and a number put into hospital under observation. Sealions bleeding from the nostrils were crawling on the beaches, and fishing was stopped in the area when traces of mercury were found inside some of the dead animals.

In July, 1978 the motor vessel *Jal Sea Condor* voyaging from Bangkok to Lagos with, among other cargo, 74 containers, radioed an S.O.S. that the crew were abandoning ship off Angola, when the engine room was under water and the vessel sinking. She subsequently sank, and the deck cargo of containers floated away. In November, 1978 it was reported from Okinawa that the motor vessel *Hima Wari Maru* was presumed sunk, and a day after the presumption, three containers and one of her life boats were found to mark the

spot. Reports of single containers sighted in the open sea are commonplace and their contents are quite unknown.

In 1973 the 2,000-ton container ship *Duke of Norfolk*, on a regular
run between Britain's east coast and Holland met storm weather,
coinciding with engine failure 20-odd miles from Holland. She lost
9,000 gallons of deadly paraquat, a weedkiller, but fatal to humans
with no known antidote, and this loss was not reported until three
days after the event. The spot where six out of eight trailers on the
deck of the ship were ripped away by the huge waves was claimed to
be near an existing continental chemicals dumping ground.

It is a commercial necessity for dangerous goods to be risked at
sea, in the air, by truck and by railroad, but care has been maintained for many years in the carriage of lethal chemicals, explosives
and radioactive substances, until the advent of the container. The
method of securing these unwieldy boxes is light hearted in the
extreme, and the labelling of dangerous cargoes including extremely
dangerous ones is considered archaic, to the point of lethal absur-
dity, both at sea and on land.

Second World War mines are as common as full stops in this book
in European waters and are frequently reported off the eastern
seaboard of the United States, but not by small ships hitting them.
This must be regarded as an inherent risk in seafaring, since little
can be done when such prolific sowing during two world wars was
done over such wide areas. It would be akin to sweeping the major
deserts for empty baked-bean cans. But a menace that should and
could be better controlled is the careless loss of floating lengths of
pipeline that can act like torpedoes to ships in storm conditions,
which frequently are featured in the casualty columns of *Lloyd's List*.
It must be admitted that a great mass of ironmongery has been
launched into orbit in the name of science, and most of it has to come
to earth sooner or later. But the total lack of understanding of the
oceans and seas being the lungs of all living creatures is growing day
by day. If airliners were to drop skips of waste food and rubbish and
drop solid objects to lighten aircraft in distress, the hue and cry
would be vociferous and immediate. That this goes on at sea on a
massive and fast growing scale is noticed by no one and the world's

Press and other means of communication report trivia and other human stupidity nearer home to encourage readership. There is no quick way of curbing this kind of pollution, and only education will make mankind conscious of his dependence upon clean seas, free of lethal floating obstructions to hazard ships occupying their business in great waters.

A çount of objects reported as seen at sea, such as tanks, buoys, pipelines, logs and prefabricated houses, between August, 1976 and June, 1979 is 70, not including floating mines. These figures would be multiplied many-fold if satellites like the Navsat, now sadly deceased, were equipped with cameras more finely tuned than presently available. As it is this satellite was of inestimable use in photographing the true position of coral reefs and reported others previously unknown, thus releasing hard pressed hydrographers from work in less remote regions. Sad to say, the best techniques are used for military purposes, and can identify a man lighting his pipe when really pressed. Equal clarity of photography around the earth is impossible, since different backgrounds give variations of reflected light, and muddy or sand-laden waters would yield little evidence photographically of dangerous floating objects, in the Western Approaches for example. But a shift of emphasis, however slight, from military surveillance to commercial overseeing would be a major step in the tracing of dangers to safe navigation.

Not long ago an aircraft over Australian waters reported a large sheet of ice, albeit in tropical waters. On closer inspection this was discovered to be a large sheet of plastic. An engineer officer who served in oil tankers up to the advent of macro tankers, which he said were devoid of any seafaring attractions, related seeing thousands of plastic bags floating down river from Bangkok to where his tanker lay at anchor. These bags came from ice creams, and were thrown into the river by children. They stopped up the cold water intake of the tanker and caused severe heating in parts of the engine room requiring constant cooling.

This small incident illustrates the great chasm between the rising generation and respect for the oceans. The number and distribution of seats in oceanography at schools throughout the world is lamentably sparse, and until children are taught the value of this complex system and the life chain it maintains, there will be no halting or diminution in pollution. The word itself has come a long way from its original meaning of "taint from mud". It would be a clean and lovely environment for us to live in if mud were the only taint we feared.

On November 3, 1979 Lloyd's reported a collision in the English Channel between the Greek coaster *Aeolian Sky* of some 6,000 tons, and the German ship *Anna Knupel*. This was at four o'clock in the morning off the Dorset coast. The ship, loaded with containers with varying contents, unable to be towed into the Solent because of her drooping bows under attack from waves generated by a 28-knot wind, sank in 30 metres of water.

"All interested authorities" were sent the cargo manifest of hazardous items, which did not include a container full of Christmas mail, gifts for 1,000 British nationals living in the Seychelles. The authority most interested should have been the Chairman of the Sea Court, sitting to find the cause of a collision when both ships had ample methods of locating each other in any visibility. The result of the adventure was that just over three months later canisters of poisonous chemicals were washed up on the Sussex coast, along with a number of dead fish and birds. The point to be noted is that this stage of the disaster only reached small print in the inner pages of newspapers. This was in spite of some of the most toxic contents being in small aluminium bottles very much like drinking cans that boys often put on the handlebars of their bicycles. Because lethal substances cannot be seen below the surface of the sea, they are forgotten and the reports to "interested authorities" are no protection for thirsty schoolboys nor for marine life.

Very few, if any, legislators in any European country could offer any cogent or comprehensive list of the whereabouts of death inducing chemicals on the seabed on the European continental shelf, and in its inshore waters. Once again, one realises that the anonymity of the container is absolute, and the natural hazards of the sea, such as a "red tide", are infinitely less destructive than those contained in magic boxes. "Red tide" is sufficiently real in its menace to have generated an international conference sponsored by the

Massachusetts Institute of Technology. It is caused by a bloom of plankton expanding in perfect conditions of warm water, conditioned by ocean currents and winds that leads to a toxic mass that turns the sea red, yellow, green or brown and kills fish by the million, and subsequently gulls, ducks and other birds which feeds on them. It is a phenomenon that has been recorded since biblical times and its most sinister characteristic is that the toxin is absorbed by shell fish but does not kill them, which is not an advantage to shell fish eaters, as the Egyptians found when Moses turned the Nile into "blood". It occurs in many parts of the world, including the southwest coast of Britain, and in Japan, where fishermen wrongly blamed industrial effluent for a fish kill that eroded their profits catastrophically.

There are thus a multitude of hazards in the ocean, and our adding to them is going to affect future generations, who will not know the origin of the menace threatening them. The "authorities" in many countries with a coastline would do well to synthesise the positions, already far from accurately known, of ships that sink with lethal cargoes, and the position of container ships when they lose deadly cargoes overboard in stormy weather. The hydrographers would give invaluable assistance in such a venture.

The *Duke of Norfolk*, losing paraquat overboard near a chemicals dumping ground, makes one hope that the keepers of this treasure house are aware of the strength of currents and the paucity of knowledge available on the rapidity and extent of rust in comparatively shallow water. Many "buried" pipelines on the seabed show the potency of rust that breaks open concrete supports releasing pipelines into the paths of ships' anchors. In the Red Sea a miniature submarine performing pipeline surveys found that it could have looped the loop under a "buried" pipeline.

There is much to discover on the seabed, which has been used as a dumping ground for unwanted chemicals ever since the Industrial Revolution. We are still discovering currents, part of the circulatory system, of the magnitude of a probable 8,000 miles; the Cromwell

Current, which is many times the mass of the Mississippi River, crosses the Pacific Ocean, carrying 40 million tons of water a second. It was only discovered in 1951, and affects the livelihood of the Japanese Islands, without a doubt, and there are other important currents to be discovered as important to us all in the days of nuclear waste, as the discovery of the circulation of blood around the human body.

The rapidity of the spread of waste and toxic substances accidentally washed or swept from the decks of ships under the sea's surface is unknown to most of the world's foremost oceanographers, much less the "interested authorities" on whom we all depend with child-like simplicity. Government succeeds government, indifferent to the increasing dangers of the spread of malignant substances by swift currents that are assumed to run on predetermined routes like railroads. The thirty-day drift of the submarine *Ben Franklin* in 1969 demonstrated finally that the Gulf Stream was not a main line train, but several swirling, colliding, meandering torrents tumbling northwards, assaulted by internal waves. The same characteristics no doubt apply to most other large ocean currents, such as the newly discovered Cromwell Current.

There is a bleak tomorrow facing our heirs and assigns, in the growing realisation among thinking people that mines and oil wells are finite in their fecundity, and their treasures cannot be wasted with impunity.

The same lack of cohesive thought and action which typifies attitudes to ocean pollution among statesmen attends the steady demise of rain forests in Africa, India and the creation of deserts by overgrazing by feral domestic animals, even in the world's ideal spot for joyful living, Hawaii. Here, the original forest has gone, and the topsoil as well, thanks to the activities of domesticated wild goats.

There is however an alternative for legislators endeavouring to catch the imagination of their citizens at the expense of catching a few votes. Neither fish, on which much of the world's population subsists, have votes, nor the vanishing bird life that has charmed navigators for centuries as they traverse the world's trade routes. Education in the quality of life is long overdue as is the inclusion of an appreciation of the beauty of wild creatures that are threatened all over the world. There is very little, if any, imploitation of sea creatures on any scale in any part of the world, with the exception perhaps of the rehabilitation of the delightful sea otter on the eastern seaboard of Canada. Perhaps one could include the cultivation of fish in the paddy fields of what was Indo-China.

The time is long overdue when we should stop looking at the ocean merely as a highway, and a playground when it is our larder, and no longer a place to be plundered at the cost of future starvation.

7. The Way Forward

We are driven to a sense of awe by the eruption of volcanoes, massive avalanches and floods. We are fascinated by accounts describing the explosion of Krakatoa in 1883. If this volcano had exploded in London, the sound would have been heard in New York. The pressure wave that followed the explosion encircled the earth seven times. The volcanic dust cloud reduced the sun's radiation by ten times, and the English Channel perceptibly rose. Such cataclysmic events are soon forgotten and are packed away in the human psyche behind the subconscious mind's defences, which act as baffles to mental breakdown and have done so since man stood erect, a geological minute ago.

The Mohole Project was seen more as a triumph over bureaucracy than one over the forces of nature. The successful retrieval of a core from a hole drilled five or six miles down through the earth's crust to prove a theory propounded by an obscure Yugoslav mathematician at the University of Zagreb is only remembered by a few academics. His study of seismic waves caused by an earthquake in 1909 led to the exciting confirmation of "continental drift", and the idea that geology was a dynamic science rather than a static one.

Explosions and their percussions and repercussions dwindle into candle-lit obscurity under the fierce light of geological upheavals over a period of 5,000 million years, when it all began. We are gradually extending the geologically minuscule period that man has stood erect. At the same time we are extending our scant knowledge of the continental jigsaw that split, to furnish our school atlases with Mercator and other colourful projections.

We have virtually no knowledge of the cataclysmic turmoils such as the penetration by Atlantic waters into the dry Mediterranean salt basin through the Straits of Gibraltar. This waterfall is too majestic for us to visualise. Huge movements of ice, of oceans and of volcanic forces of unimaginable power, burying tropical forests and rendering a huge range of creatures extinct in a short period, created our present sources of motive power and much of our ill-distributed wealth. The birth of every American child is fifty times more of a disaster for the world than the birth of each Indian child. If you take consumption of steel as a measure of overall consumption, you find that the birth of each American child is 300 times more of a disaster for the world than the birth of each Indonesian child.

We are wasting the legacy given to us by the quick demise of flesh and fibre at a rate and pace that bring the extinction of mankind closer as each year passes. As scientists, geologists and oceanographers reveal the earth's history, a greater realisation of the precariousness of our existence is sombrely unfolded. Pollution, whether by chemicals or oils of varying kinds, is the result of a total lack of comprehension of the scale of magnitude of the loss of precious treasure from the emptying mines and oil coffers that we are plundering so wantonly. The oil loss by spillage over the past 20 years could mobilise a vast army, but could also have warmed, clothed and fed millions of people.

The oil companies of the world consider themselves beyond criticism, which is a dangerous stance in the circumstances we face. That the maritime disasters resulting in the carriage of oils and gases across the oceans are not in many instances due to the fault or priority of tanker operators, is beyond doubt. But the glib reiteration of absolute blamelessness and the clinging in the face of a huge increase in oil pollution to the contention that oil has seeped from the seabed for aeons of time, do them a disservice. The managers of big well-run fleets of tankers are potent allies in what is now a battle for survival. They are in a most responsible position to make careless ownership uneconomic, which will be a major step in halting the present race to disaster.

Too often the emphasis is on the amount of oil carried safely in relation to that lost. The conferences called after a major spillage

13) **Pumping oil ashore from the** *Amoco Cadiz*, **Portsall, Brittany. (Press Association)**

turn out to be descriptions of brilliant salvage operations, rather than an examination into the causes of tragic losses of precious fuel in a world facing the possibilities of an ice age exacerbated by a drying out of our fuel bins. The lead taken by Exxon in refusing to charter sub-standard ships with sub-standard officers is a responsible step of great magnitude and impact. It will reap great rewards for many industries as well as prolong the life of many sea creatures and animals and birds. The big oil-carrying fleets are a bastion against a rapidly declining range of seafaring skills that start with bad management in shipping offices and spread to ill-trained ship's officers and carelessness that would be labelled as criminal lunacy if it were on land or in the air where the effect is very easily observed. If the losses of commodities that are considered acceptable today were to have occurred during the Second World War, wholly to one side or the other, they would have led to a shortening of hostilities. Statistics blindfold comprehension of orders of magnitude, and can be manoeuvred to prove trends or disprove them.

"The Decade of the Ocean" mooted in Washington in 1969 heralded the worst phase of pollution the world has ever experienced, both on land and at sea. Writing to *The Times* of London on November 5, 1970 the late Sir Francis Chichester said, "I have just returned from a 4,600-mile try-out sail in my *Gipsy Moth V* to the Mediterranean and back.

"Time after time we sailed through patches of or slicks of oil film on the surface. Seas coming aboard the yacht left clots of black oil on the deck and stained the sails. I noticed signs or effects of oil at intervals all the way from the Solent to Gibraltar and in the Mediterranean itself, between Gibraltar and Majorca.

"I mention this because I think it is probably more noticeable from a small low yacht than from a steamer. Does it mean that in time, if it continues to increase, the oil effect will kill life at sea?"

In December, 1970 the Food and Agriculture Organisation of the U.N. spent nine days in Rome discussing pollution between 300 environmentalists. The Press release stated: "The urgency of such a meeting is emphasised almost daily by the discovery of new kinds of pollutants and widening sources of contamination in addition to oil spillages."

In spite of the words of President Nixon in 1969, it is all too apparent that there were no benefits for the people of the world in connection with the oceans, seas, rivers and lakes on this tiny planet. The coming decade will be infinitely worse if the present trends are permitted to continue, and there are no signs of their being deflected or reversed.

The lifting of the veil of secrecy that continuously hides the enormity of carelessness by ill-trained Masters and deck officers of ships carrying pollutants, would be a most important step towards ultimate success in curbing spillages. In January 1980, the 61,000-tonne deadweight oil tanker *Scenic* caused spillages at Sullom

**14) The sheer size of the wrecked supertanker *Amoco Cadiz* is apparent in
this bow view of the stricken supertanker. (Press Association)**

Voe, in the Shetlands, at the major oil terminal there. The Deputy
Director of Ports and Harbours at Sullom Voe wrote to the Greek
owners, Nereus Shipping, to say that this and other ships of the same
ownership were no longer welcome at the terminal. The reason given
was that the ships had been navigating variously, without proper
charts, inefficient manning, overloading, crewmen smoking in for-
bidden areas and carrying fire-fighting and life-saving equipment far
below acceptable standards. She proved to be so overloaded that she
was 18 inches too deep in the water, and 3,000 tonnes of crude oil had
to be pumped back. The Department of Trade Marine Inspector
was called in and found a lifeboat engine not working, and round the
accommodation alleyways the ship was in a "generally filthy state".

Hours after she was finally cleared to sail, there was an engine room explosion. The charterers were Union Oil of California. B.P., mindful of Shetland Islanders' feelings on the maintenance of clean shores, is planning a computer check on the ships time charters, on its history, culminating in inspectors checking these findings. The chartering of ships unseen is patently at the centre of the whole problem of slowing the catastrophic rate of spillage.

The steps being taken by B.P. and in the U.S.A. by Exxon in their refusal to accept sub-standard ships or crews for charter is the boldest step yet, well above the ineffectual arena of politics and into that of a cleaner ocean in the 1980's. But this care cannot embrace the lunacy of large tankers at anchor being engulfed in flames by being hit by small ships in the hands of incompetents.

This is another reason for the promotion of Sea Courts all over the globe, to find the ill-run ships and guilty owners with immediacy thus giving full impact on legislators and the public.

The world must look to the operators of big tanker fleets whose sense of responsibility can meet such a huge problem, by pressure on governments. They are jealous of their reputations as efficient seafarers and thus will be listened to.

The Mercantile Marine Act of 1850 in England was designed to protect the private rights of shipowners, in the face of public demand for safety at sea. The changes since then have been dramatic but suffocating in the administration of Maritime Law. Amateur shipowners are being protected by long delay, so that their legal representatives can play havoc with the memories of witnesses long after the accidents. The law has become a benefit to the guilty and an impetus to the upward graph of accidents and pollution in the oceans. The guilty escape public opprobrium.

In 1871, Germany started a laudable, workable and effective system of legal "fire brigades". They were called "Sea Courts" and consist of two Maritime Lawyers with an "Interrogator", usually a retired Admiral. Each protagonist, following an accident in German waters, has an advocate, to see that fair play is done.

In this way the guilty are shown up soon after the event, measured in hours, and their accident inducing actions or inactions are quickly recorded becoming healthy, topical, public knowledge. The measure in British and other Maritime Courts is in months and frequently years, avoiding public condemnation when it is most effective, with the accident still in the public mind.

Leaving the problem of pollution in these hands, it is wise to look into alternative methods of transporting fossil fuels and dangerous chemicals. The steady loss of containers from storm harassed ships points at design criteria that have not included the power of wind-driven water attacking deck cargoes. These containers are packed with all manner of substances, varying from illicit drugs to cyanide and lethal gases, with no indication of the contents on the outside.

An alternative method of ocean transport is the sailing ship, which is an increasingly attractive economic proposition. It has been shown to be as a viable alternative to oil and steam driven ships by the use of sails on a jack-up oil rig under tow, giving the tow an overall extra half knot. This is of great value both in saving costs and avoiding impending bad weather, for example. The sails, the largest in the world, are 180 feet high and 75 feet wide at the foot and have an expanse of 6,750 square feet, the shape of things to come. When the wind is directly astern a second sail is used, and speed increases of up to 2 knots have been achieved, towing these unwieldy structures. In the Chesapeake Bay off Norfolk, Virginia, a Captain Lane Briggs, owner and operator of a conventional steel tug has, by the fitting of two masts with gaff rigged sails, reduced fuel bills by 30%. It increases speed by 1.6 knots and has been proven efficient over the past several years towing barges, using sail in every favourable wind.

Following wind tunnel tests, the Nippon Kokan K.K. installed synthetic fabric sails in a 77-ton model of the 460,000-ton tanker, the *Daioh*, saving 10% in fuel costs during the sea trials. Fishermen in Brittany finding the increase in oil and gasoline prices was denuding profit on long haul trips, have turned to sails as the answer; with auxiliary motors they will consume six times less fuel, and save each boat 230,000 litres of fuel a week. The idea has been grasped by the French Merchant Navy and a national agency has been set up to further the idea in bigger ships. In the U.S.S.R. at Nikolayev in the Ukraine a symposium on wind-powered merchant ships listened to a description of a 60,000-ton cargo ship driven by sail.

The most searching enquiry into the dynamics of the sailing ship with those aviation implanted upon them, was undertaken by Wilhelm Prolss, a German aerodynamics engineer. He found the old sailing ships grossly inefficient in relation to aircraft wings and in most other considerations and presented his findings to the Schiff-bau Institut in Hamburg. They were astonished to contemplate the plans for a sailing ship with 200-foot masts devoid of any stays, lines or shrouds to anchor them. But the concept was impressive in its simplicity, a 17,000-ton ship capable of 24 knots. The vessel has three masts with Dacron sails and steel yards, all set by remote control from the bridge. The vessel has auxiliary engines, a gas turbine and two lesser diesels for manoeuvring in calm seas or in port areas. The Prolss system proved to be superior to 12- and 7-metre sailing yachts and not surprisingly to the beautiful old five-masted *Preussen*.

Research into three-masted sailing ships on the lines of the Prolss experiments are in hand in the United States, on Priest Lake, Idaho.

The increasing efficiency of weather routing of ships will increase the acceptability of the "Dynaship" principle, to date starved of funds to built a full-size ship, but with each oil spillage and each rise in the price of oil, the time approaches more and more urgently for sail to supplement fossil-fuel-driven ships.

All notions of romance have been driven from the oceans, and the elegance of ships is now part of history. A return to the merchant ship driven by sophisticated automated sails would appeal strongly to the many frustrated seafarers all over the world, to the ultimate benefit of mankind envisaged so ironically by President Nixon at the dawn of the last "decade of the oceans".

The latest trend in turning ships into extensions of port facilities is the fashion for container ships with two gantry cranes running over the length of the vessel, as though it were a factory floor, to make loading faster than shore facilities can deal with. In the early days of diamond extraction off the "Skeleton" coast of South West Africa, barges were being loaded with mining machinery in the simulation of a land operation. One of these huge monstrosities had to be tacked out of Cape Town harbour as if it were a Tudor galleon. A look at any illustrated scale of sea states issued by a variety of establishments gives such hybrid manifestations the life expectancy of a butterfly. Stress of weather has become a totally remote consideration in the minds of many naval architects practising today, and they are unlikely to be aware of the steady loss of containers from the decks of ships that seem designed to attract large bodies of fast-moving wind-driven water.

The work of dedicated scientists in the pursuit of accuracy in long, medium and short term damage to marine life is frequently spurned by legislators for purely political reasons. This occurred, but was observed to have happened in time for correction, in the case of the *Metula* in the Straits of Magellan. A highly professional appraisal of the damage done by the 47,000 tons of light Arabian crude oil and 4,000 odd tons of "Bunker C" oil, spilled by the stricken ship, resulted in a sober and accurate appraisal by Dr. Jenifer Baker, of the Orielton Field Centre in Pembroke, Wales. This report, made on behalf of Tovalop, the international tanker group, opined that the results of the spill were not severe in terms of being widespread or in the devastation of marine and bird life, including penguins, on any great scale. It was made by a marine biologist of international repute and wide field experience in connection with coastal damage by oils.

The report was challenged by an American consultant, a chemist, who admitted that the *Metula* was the first oil spillage that he had ever seen. He was observed to walk along the foreshore counting dead birds and later published a report extrapolating the figures for the birds he found in terms of a considerable length of coast line. He thus assessed 40,000 dead cormorants and penguins whereas the British report assessed the count as 1,500 which was subsequently confirmed by another report by the Patagonian Institute. It was later surmised that the American report was a political one in connection with the desirability of oil terminals for very large tankers on the Eastern American Seaboard, then under discussion in Congress.

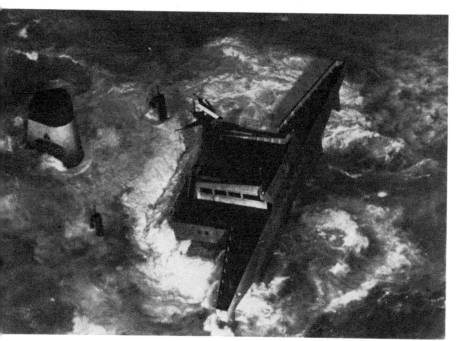

15) The rear bridge section of the *Amoco Cadiz* emerges from the water. (Associated Press)

A similar act of cynicism occurred in California when the Administration called for a report on the effect of industrial effluent on fish life in Californian coastal waters. The report, again made by expert marine biologists, stressed that the fish were healthy, and larger than they had ever been *because of* the effluent. The report was rejected by the Administration.

Considerable studies were made following the *Argo Merchant* disaster on December 15, 1976, 27 miles south of Nantucket Island, the main finding being that the long term effects on the small creatures at the bottom of the chain of marine life were impossible to assess, due as much to their migratory habits as to their small size. The interesting fact was that the ship grounded in December, 1976, and the court hearing, that established the guilty party, was held on February 8, *1980*. Even after six months, public and legislative interest was on the wane, and by the end of three years, few people could recall even the vessel's name. The judgement that the vessel was unsafe, carried obsolete charts, and was 18 miles off course when she struck the sand bar, has come much too late to make the slightest impact on other seafarers as a warning, or to legislators, to comprehend the levity with which internationally agreed safety standards are treated at sea. This is one further example of the extraordinary and unjustifiable delays in bringing guilty parties to book, following an environmental catastrophe or heavy loss of life. In no other field of transport are such inordinate delays tolerated. Much of the fault in this country lies in the staunch efforts of government officials to muzzle all statements from those who could and should disclose irregularities at the time of the accident when topical reports made by competent sea courts assessors would be of real value as a deterrent.

With delays in Court hearings on this scale, underwriters who have to meet the claims generated by the "accident" can formulate no defence worthy of the name, and once again the guilty go unscathed when public attention would be as healthy a weapon as it is in aviation accidents. The insurance industry has been leaned upon too heavily, and too long with its defences demolished by the demise of the "Captains' Register" at Lloyd's and the length of delay between accident and Court of Law.

The notion that "time is money" set the stage for many tragedies at sea and most of the pollution threatens many species of animals, birds, coastal fish and plants as well as the cleanliness of beaches. Short cuts to "catch the tide" or to save fuel are a major source of "accidents", emphasised by the *Torrey Canyon* being followed by many others, including the use of the Agulhas Current off the East African coast to save time and fuel but to hazard ships meeting episodic waves, to risk breaking their backs, or worse. The slowing down of ships, particularly in congested waters, would do nothing but good in this respect, bearing in mind the tendency of big ships to "squat" at low speeds. But the use of sails, which were successful in the early days of steam as a useful alternative to general cargo work, will be an effective and much cheaper alternative for the carriage of goods by sea, leaving bulk cargo ships to less congested sea lanes.

Before touching on alternative fuels and methods of saving fossil fuels it is as well to understand the nature of pollution and the stage reached by knowledgeable marine biologists in assessing real or imagined damage by spilt oils and chemicals.

The most telling information coming from these people is not what they know of the long-term effects of varying grades of oil pollution on marine life, but what they do not know. The lack of such knowledge is not for want of zeal or of appreciation of the urgent nature of the task, but more the complexity of the interaction of various sorts of marine life in inshore tidal areas where plant life can be severely damaged or killed. These tidal waters are of vital propagation to the procreation and welfare of many forms of marine life, most of which are interwoven in the utmost complexity and form the basis of a life chain upon which larger fish depend.

Migratory marine animals in the open sea are quite different, and no one on earth can claim to have any knowledge of the long-term effect of oils, mercury or other chemical pollution on them, or on the larger fish that graze on them. Small samples of plankton can be obtained by the use of "Nansen bottles", which trap them at pre-determined depths, but this on a scale with any real meaning would be akin to trapping bees in the Himalayas during summer months from helicopters, to determine a commonality of damage from airborne industrial effluent from the cities of the plains. Yet the welfare and rate of reproduction of plankton and krill, its bigger brothers and sisters, is as vital to fish life as the bee is in the cross-fertilization of pollen from plant to plant. It will be many years before sufficient funds are available for marine biologists to make an assessment of the long-term changes or damage done by spillage of oils and chemicals, to plankton and other small organisms on which the fish community depend completely.

The facts concerning the collision of the *Aeolian Sky* carrying highly toxic chemicals are obscure, and will emerge in low circulation technical journals many months after the news value of the events has been lost. Lethal chemicals packaged in canisters attractive to children being washed up on the English South Coast are enough

16) The *Olympic Bravery*, smashed on the rocks of Brittany, January 1976, the most expensive insurance write-off in history. (Popper)

cause for alarm for a Minister to go and visit the site. What is more alarming is that substances that the ship's manifest disclose she did not carry are also among the 1,000 canisters driven ashore. There is therefore another vessel or container on the seabed releasing its toxic cargo into the mêlée.

The time has come to escort ships with explosive or toxic cargoes whilst in congested waters prone to collision and sudden stress of weather. Responsible Ministers must know the whereabouts of ships carrying dangerous cargoes around coastal areas. Salvage tugs and small naval vessels can act as escorts. The frequency of sinkings and loss of deck cargoes is sufficiently well recorded to give ample support to this contention. Our scale of values on the costs of such a service is totally distorted, as the Spanish holiday camp tragedy when a liquid gas tanker exploded with great loss of life proved. The cost of the endeavours to salvage dangerous cargo from the *Aeolian Sky* must be measured in terms of the danger to divers, limited in time to minutes diving in slack water, to poisoned fish and birds, and to the threat to children touching the objects washed onto beaches, against the small cost of an escort vessel. Ships carrying dangerous cargoes should be painted red and carry prominent lights to warn off candidates for collisions.

On October 15, 1979, a French warship reported a container 3 metres by 4 metres drifting in the Channel, a danger to navigation. No-one knows what ship this container fell from, nor its contents. Nor does anyone know whether container losses overboard are reported each time they occur. It *is* known that insurance Under-writers are increasingly unwilling to grant insurance cover on deck cargoes in containers. This sort of pollution is an increasing menace with no braking mechanism anywhere in the world to observe or halt its increase.

A recapitulation of the problems facing the inhabitants of this tiny jewel suspended in the void is not difficult to assemble. Husbanding the harvests of immense geological upheavals that trapped flora and fauna millions of years ago is an awesome responsibility. It has been and is being treated with a flippancy and lack of foresight that are a route to a bleak future for all living creatures. We have nowhere else to go in the firmament for minerals and hydrocarbons except under the keels of ships and under our own feet. Mining, in geological terms, is in its infancy, and so is our thinking in terms of the potential of the mines and wells available to us through the pioneering work of oilmen and geologists. That they are finite is beyond question. The speed with which we have devoured these rare gifts will be a matter for criticism by our children's children. What we do to correct what appears to many as an irreversible trend is the debate we must face.

We have much to learn about the intricacies of our planet, and more as to how to preserve them. Are an elite of power seekers plundering the innocent masses? Is it a cohesive co-ordinated plan by a few against the many? The answer must be a negative one. The ordinary citizens in any country yearn for stability to rear their

17) The crew of the Greek tanker *Global Hope* dot the snow covered decks of the huge ship run aground in Massachusetts Bay, in February 1978, waiting for rescue by US Coast Guard helicopters. (Associated Press)

children and grandchildren with sufficient food, warmth and stimuli to create comfort allied to a sense of fulfilment. The carriage of lethal chemicals in inshore waters is hideously dangerous, and there are many recent cases to choose from to demonstrate the seriousness of the present chaos of no-one knowing where ships are and what they carry, at any given moment.

As Dr. Schumacher pointed out to an indifferent world, we are using up oil, coal, gas and the rest on such a vast scale, man is treating them as capital, not income. No enterprise can survive on such a philosophy indefinitely. One can feel confident that his prognosis only took into account the extraction of fossil and other fuels and not the profligate waste in spillage and inefficient combustion that occur on the surface. This point leads to another even more sombre one. The burning of fossil fuels will release enough carbon dioxide over the next two decades to more than double the amount in the atmosphere. No one can predict how quickly this gas will be absorbed by the ocean. Nor can anyone predict what effect this increase will have on the world's climate. The surface of the oceans is its most important component, and is not one to be trifled with with impunity, as we are doing today so unthinkingly. We are living for the moment with scant consideration for the comfort or safety of our great-grandchildren. No other generation has put the existence of the race in jeopardy and been so indifferent to reality.

Experts in many fields of chemistry, ship construction, hydrography, waves and currents, who have studied their subjects and practised them in the field are ignored by legislators. Ministers who could use such depth of knowledge are ignorant of its existence and thus legislation complicates the chaos rather than achieving any clarification. Successive Administrations produce Ministers backed by permanent civil servants with no knowledge of the usages of ocean-going ships and traffic lanes in congested waters become so complicated as to be ignored by even the best-managed ships. Much legislation is incomprehensible to shipowners and operators alike and ships' officers spend valuable time sifting forms that give employment to remote civil servants to give placebo answers to angry Members of Parliament.

Nothing has changed in the past ten years to halt the steady increase of lost lives and lost cargoes, the contamination of the oceans and the threat to the most endangered species, sanity. Until those put in power in democratic countries understand that dedicated oceanographers and hydrographers should be consulted before voters, the waste of the earth's dwindling treasures will increase. We are not the sufferers, but we sentence those who come after us to a bleak and ugly world for want of ordinary foresight. A news-hungry public is quickly indifferent to yesterday's disasters and the human psyche survives by wiping out a superfluity of painful memories. We must find quick means to reduce disasters at sea before we are in the midst of a bankrupt world.

World-Wide Ship Casualty Table 1978

These tables of total losses and serious casualties to powered sea-going vessels of 500 tons and over were compiled by the casualty Branch of Lloyd's Intelligence Department

ACCORDING TO COUNTRY

Flag	Losses No.	Losses GRT	Serious No.	Serious GRT
Algerian	1	1598		
American	6	60055	4	35417
Argentine	1	2124	2	12293
Austrian			1	5997
Australian	1	1616		
Brazilian	1	1213	1	3233
British	5	13663	4	4937
Bulgarian			1	6260
Canadian	1	3911	2	6809
Chilean	1	35048	2	11820
Chinese			2	19811
Colombian			1	5248
Cuban			1	3888
Cyprus	23	62673	6	34961
Danish	1	1399	1	982
Dubai			1	6753
Dutch	2	2318	1	3520
East German	1	1744		
French	2	19515	2	17543
Finnish	1	1217		
Greek	68	582141	35	397344
Honduran	2	3324		
Hungarian			1	2741
Indian	3	24848	4	80218
Iranian	3	10524	3	23164
Irish			1	5285
Italian	4	12271	2	53651
Japanese	9	21415	6	25911
Lebanese	3	3146	2	1461
Liberian	7	164665	12	437177
Libyan			1	10965
Maltese			1	999
Moroccan	1	8748		
Neth. Antilles	1	543		
Norwegian	2	9593	1	2117
Pakistani			1	8991
Panama	43	180288	19	133171
Philippine	5	8963	4	7791
Polish			2	14032
Portuguese	1	803		
Russian	1	1350	5	32224
Seychelles	1	7920		
Sharjah	1	8500		
Singapore	5	24246	7	107911
South African	1	630		
South Korean	7	10268	1	8871
Spanish	5	6567	5	37697
Swedish	3	4384	2	25297
Taiwan			1	2770
Thai			2	3734
Tunisian			1	4237
Turkish	1	1127	1	9899
West German	2	37634	1	23414
Yugoslav			3	21685
Totals	226	1352000	158	1662227

SIZE (tons)

SIZE (tons)	Losses No.	Losses GRT	Serious No.	Serious GRT
500–999	40	29661	16	13175
1000–4999	112	248848	54	153812
5000–9999	46	361831	42	317636
10000–19999	14	194276	31	437794
20000–29999	5	118852	7	169202
30000+	9	398732	8	570608
Totals	226	1352000	158	1662227

AGE

AGE	Losses No.	Losses GRT	Serious No.	Serious GRT
0–4	9	150502	22	392798
5–9	26	165117	34	505270
10–14	34	240181	26	291529
15–19	34	294148	23	177208
20–24	63	323110	34	213057
25+	60	178942	19	82365
Totals	226	1352000	158	1662227

TYPE

TYPE	Losses No.	Losses GRT	Serious No.	Serious GRT
General cargo	169	618375	99	504009
General cargo/ wine tanker			1	4237
Oil tanker	18	478816	6	276476
Oil/chemical tanker	2	20785	5	237763
Chemical tanker	3	5596		
Trawler	5	4685	2	2645
Liquefied gas tanker	3	2634	3	4148
M.F.Y.	5	7904	1	1552
Ro-ro	6	15322	5	38589
Ore carrier			2	24474
Tug/supply vesel	2	1292	1	865
Bulk carrier	10	150183	25	513039
Bulk carrier/ cable layer	1	7676		
Container vessel			5	45600
Trawler/fish factory			1	3888
Fish carrier	1	1598	1	3308
Ferry			1	1608
Barge carrier	1	37134		
Totals	226	1352000	158	1662227

Bibliography

The Shape of Ships	Hutchinson
The Admiralty Chart	Hollis and Carter
Krakatoa	Secker and Warburg
The Sun Beneath the Sea	Scribners
Victory Ships and Tankers	David and Charles
Oil and Water	William Kimber
Geology Resources and Society	Freeman
Experience and Behaviour	Pelican Books
Waves and Beaches	Doubleday
Knights Modern Seamanship	Van Nostrand Reinhold
The Telegraph	Monthly
Lloyd's List and Shipping Gazette	
Safety at Sea	Monthly
The Times	
The Guardian	
The Observer	